THEM AND US

THEM and US

CULT THINKING AND THE TERRORIST THREAT

ARTHUR J. DEIKMAN, M.D.

Foreword by DORIS LESSING

BAY TREE PUBLISHING
Berkeley, California

Bay Tree books may be purchased for business or promo-
tional use or for special sales. Please contact: Special Sales
Department, Bay Tree Publishing, 721 Creston Road,
Berkeley, CA 94708.

Library of Congress Control Number: 2003109934
ISBN: 0-9720021-2-X

Cover design by Twin Engine
Interior design and composition by BookMatters

04 05 06 07   5 4 3 2

To Henry and Gertrude Mandelbaum

Contents

Foreword by Doris Lessing   ix

Acknowledgements   xvii

Introduction   1

1   **The Cult Mirror**   5
    A Common Story · The Dependency Fantasy

2   **Hugh and Clara: A Case History**   14

3   **Compliance with the Group**   54
    The Power of Groups · The Threat of Conflicting
    Loyalties · The Conversion Experience · Oppression
    by Censure · Degrees of Dependence · Career
    Realities and Cult Demands · Corporate Culture
    or Corporate Cult? · Self-Deception and Compliance

4   **Dependence on a Leader**   74
    Making Ourselves Small · The Use and Abuse
    of Hierarchies · Looking for Leaders · The Fantasy
    Leader · The Leader's Fantasy · When Facts Don't
    Count · The Draw of Idealism · Up and Down the

Corporate Ladder · Unintended Consequences of
Power · Submission and Security · The Rewards of
Surrender · The Cult Continuum · Dangers in Psycho-
therapy · Worrisome Practices in Psychoanalytic
Institutes · Blind Followers and Blind Leaders ·
The Power of a Higher Authority

5 **Devaluing the Outsider** 107

Devaluation and Projection · The Confidence of the
Righteous · The Power of Boundaries · How the Media
Portrays "Them" · The Cost of Devaluation · Seeing
the Enemy Abroad

6 **Avoiding Dissent** 126

Unspoken Boundaries in the Media · Selective
Reporting · Advertising's Covert Indoctrination ·
Officially Sanctioned Truths · Self-Censorship in
the Media · Wanting to Believe Doesn't Make It So ·
Who Gets to Choose? · Reinforcing Belief · The
Power of Secrecy · The Benefits of Being Contradicted

7 **Escape from Cult Thinking** 150

My Own (and Your) Cult Thinking · Official Self-
Deception · Illusory Debates · Fostering Dissent ·
An Uncomfortable Process · The Eye-Level World ·
Gandhi's Experiment · Distinguishing the Moral ·
Going Beyond Dependence

8 **The Terrorist Threat** 170

What "They" Think · What "We" Think · Looking for
Causes · Looking for Solutions · Coda

Notes 187

Index 199

Foreword

This book first appeared when David Koresh at Waco, and Jim Jones at Jonestown, were recent events and of illustrative value. Research had been, and since has been, going on into cults and cultish behavior, and how we are all influenced by peer pressure. It is fair to say that few people who think at all have not given thought to cults, those they have been in, are in, or might join. Arthur Deikman's prime and particular contribution, apart from drawing attention to the problem, was to point out how much cultish behavior goes on unrecognized, in, for instance, business life or in apparently harmless organizations, religious or philanthropic.

It is useful to ask oneself the question: Do I feel superior because I belong to . . . whatever it is? Do I look down on people outside? Perhaps the most easily seen feature of a cult is expressed in the phrase: *We* are better than *them*. It is salutary to recognize how often in a day we feel disapproval or superiority, matching ourselves with "outsiders," who are black, white, fat, old, young, men, women, Moslems, Jews, Palestinians. Some of Arthur Deikman's conclusions provoked anger. It is not pleasant to be told that one's dear, reputable, ethical club or party sometimes behaves like the most intolerant cult.

Since September 2001, our perspective has shifted, and the talk is all of terrorism. A new chapter in this book discusses al Qaeda as a cult. With such a wide lens an attempt at definitions must surely be made. The accepted criteria used to define a cult also describes a nation at war or under threat. What then is the immediate usefulness of being on the lookout for cult behavior, thinking of groups or a religion like Jim Jones' Peoples Temple, when your country has embraced that basic, not to say most primitive of stances: "My country, right or wrong." Or, but this is usually the cry of extreme political parties: "He who is not with us is against us."

We are now using the word terrorist as once, and not long ago, we talked of "communists," as an all-purpose, all-embracing evil. Or even, in some parts of the world, though hard to understand in others, the word "liberal." In South Africa, under Apartheid, that was not an epithet you would want to attract.

One kind of terrorist may be dismissed from this study at once: summed up by the immortal lines of Sir John Harington (sixteenth century):

Treason doth never prosper: what's the reason?
For if it do prosper, none dare call it treason.

Not a few of today's leaders, Israel's for one, have been called terrorists. It doesn't do to be too hasty with one's definitions.

Another kind, a minority, but notable, is the young person—usually male but not always—of good family, or even rich, who becomes violently opposed to what has made him. This has been called the "Younger Son Syndrome." The Red Brigades of Italy, and the Bader-Meinhof Gang of Germany, were of this type. In my belief it was the brutal anarchy of wartime Italy and Germany that created them, but that is another question. Lenin was an example: from a cultured family that verged on the nobility, he turned against his origins, was a true terrorist—that is, advocating terrorism as a policy—and evolved into a revered leader. For a time. Bin Laden comes from a very rich family. He is no representative of the poor and downtrodden railing against the rich. Typically, while execrating the indulgences of The Great Satan, a good many of his followers, if not himself, have become addicted to the fleshpots. These types of malcontent, or revolutionary, or reformer, are easily spotted and understood.

The movements now often called "terrorist" are sometimes vast, may comprise whole populations. They have little in common with terrorists like bin Laden's specially trained terrorist groups.

In 1986 I went to Pakistan with a group involved with the plight of Afghan refugees from the Russian invasion. Around the towns, but particularly around Peshawar, on the border, were refugee camps full of women and girls. The men were inside Afghanistan fighting. The women and girls were prisoners in the camps, monitored by the mullahs, who are ignorant men without education. The girls got no education at all. The boys, however, did: they were taught, day in, day out, to recite the Koran, by these same mullahs. And that is all they were taught. Visitors to the camps or to the streets of Peshawar were surrounded by flocks of lively, if undernourished, boys of all ages, clamoring for a book. "Please give me a book," or a pen or a piece of paper. They wanted to learn. They knew that beyond the confines of the tents or hovels that made up the camps was a world they could aspire to, with education. But an education for the modern world was not what they were getting. Delightful boys, funny, clever, and heartbreaking. Soon they became the Taliban. Ignorant, obsessive, fanatical, often cruel, these frightening young men had been those attractive children. And there they still are, set aside, and they have no place or function in the modern world. Educated as the poor have been in Islam for centuries, by no more than a ritual chanting of the Koran, they might just as well be fourteenth-century people. These young men, soon to be middle-aged, are described as terrorists. They were the direct product of the Russian invasion, which the Afghans well named The Catastrophe. They are still a danger. Given the opportunity they might rise up in some mindless surge of destruction, as they did when they blew up the great statues of the Buddha. They would go back to persecuting women. But that is what they were taught. They were never given an alternative.

How can one equate these with the dedicated, specialist operatives of the al Qaeda?

In parts of Africa where Islam is merely a rumor are children, including girls, who are the result of murderous genocidal wars. Like the Taliban they will find no role in the modern world because they have no education.

They yearn to learn. Anyone visiting Africa knows how they beg for books, paper, pens, anything. "Please send us to school. Please send us a teacher." There they are, potential armies ready for the first demagogue who will give them identity and self-respect by enrolling them in a party, an army. Anywhere in the poor world, the developing nations, if you look close, there they are, the uneducated children for whom the modern world will always be a dream.

You cannot legislate against terrorist groups once they come into being, but you can prevent terrorists from coming into being. A good modern education is the solution. Some of the billions we spend on weapons and war would do it. But I doubt if the people who wield the weapons, and who make money out of them, would listen to the argument.

I saw this. I was by chance in Ireland on that shore across the bay from where Lord Mountbatten was murdered. The murder of a political opponent may be described as a gallant act of war. I looked down from my hotel bedroom and saw thirty or so street kids, poor kids, marching around under banners and posters—homemade bits of cardboard—exulting in the murder of the English enemy. The point is, this was before the European Community poured money into Ireland. Those kids now would not be fodder for the I.R.A. recruiting officers. Then, they would have to grow up to join the I.R.A. They had no other role model for brave heroes. And once inside the I.R.A. they were stuck. One does not say to a fanatical organization, "Sorry, I made a mistake. I want to take my exams and become an engineer."

Why is it is so difficult to solve and soothe the hurts of Ireland? A member of the I.R.A. or Protestant action squads is a hero. They have earned respect from their fellows for the murders they have committed and the kneecaps they have blown off. Disband these organizations and what are they? Untrained, uneducated, they are fit to become clerks or street cleaners. It is a mistake to forget, when a youngster joins a Cause, an army, a cult, follows a leader, that he is given an identity. A kid on a street corner in Los Angeles or Rio or Lagos is a social nuisance, given as much respect as a stray dog, but then he puts on a uniform and becomes somebody. A badge will do. A T-shirt. The most common cry of our street kids in Britain is for respect. "I beat him up because he gave me *dis*." Disrespect.

Any of the kinds of people I have mentioned may be called terrorists. What they have in common is the need for an enemy.

And now the worst of peace's enemies, anathematized every time President Bush or Prime Minister Blair makes a speech. Everywhere we are told are the groups of Moslem hardliners, biding their time in hiding, waiting to attack. These men—and some women—have had a religious upbringing, but it is striking how often the relatives or friends of some discovered fanatic will say: "He was quite normal, a delightful fellow until suddenly . . ." What was sudden was religious conversion, from ordinary congregational religion, religion shared with your community, to the membership of an elite group.

Some extremists, of any persuasion, are obviously psychopaths. It seems to me an insufficiently noticed fact that a person may be quite mad, but if he or she is in a political or religious context, then no one sees it.

Instructive now to read Dostoyevsky's *The Devils* (sometimes translated as *The Possessed)*, a story set in provincial Russia about a terrorist cult. This group existed for destruction, the creation of anarchy, of fear. Why? Just for the hell of it. Since this book was written, we have become familiar with killings or mayhem for its own sake. The enjoyment of destruction is deep in the human psyche, and of evidence there is plenty. The Red Guards of China: accounts record the relish in destroying everything from productive orchards, to temples, to art treasures. Cromwell's men in Britain relished destroying religious art. King Henry VIII's men thoroughly enjoyed wrecking monasteries. My question is, how often is this deep and sick need to destroy being fed under the guise of ideology? When a cult calls itself Cleansers of the Pure Flame (an invented name) and then kills, tortures and burns, blows up buildings and burns crops, it is surely time we asked, not "Are they sincere in their beliefs?" but "How much of it is for kicks, for fun, for pleasure?" I do not doubt that al Qaeda groups are sincere in their abhorrence of the West, but if there were not martyrdom, murder and the infliction of pain as part of their agenda, would they have so many recruits? And we must remember the pleasure people take in secrecy, the taking of oaths, knowing themselves to be part of invisible brotherhood, being "in the know." The belief that you are one of a powerful minority and in the right in the eyes of God or of History or your revered leader, is seductive, like a drug. The memoirs of some spy—there have been so many—tells what a thrill he got out of knowing he was seen as an ordinary, not very interesting person, "but what I knew could destroy them all."

The leaders of al Qaeda are not mad: they have a different worldview—so different it is difficult not to despair of the two sides coming to an understanding.

Outside our chief Moslem Mosque, in London, at the time of the September 11 attack, a Moslem youth was filmed saying, "Did you see all those yuppies flying out of the windows? It was so funny." He meant the people jumping to their deaths. One's blood freezes at what is revealed here. First, the language of the dispossessed: the word "yuppies." Envy, powerfully part of the hatred of The Great Satan. And then, those people working in the World Trade Center, and they included Moslems, were enemies, not human, their deaths were "funny." The youth was rebuked by religious superiors, but the chilling evidence is there, on record, and to be learned from.

"We and They. Us and Them." "He who is not with us is against us."

The main plank of cultish behavior is that the outsider, the person not on your side, is demonized. Cultish? It goes back thousands of years to our origins in the tribe, the clan: cults, nations, warring armies. "My country right or wrong."

And now, in a world as threatening and full of hatred as ours, what is to be done?

As always, there must be an appeal to the moderates on all sides. There are moderates and peacelovers and people of goodwill and it is essential to remember that when leaders posture and threaten, the voices of common sense are always softer than the noisy rhetoric of extremism.

In Britain there are organizations of moderate Moslems who dislike and disown the Moslem extremists. They are informed, educated, intelligent, and have solutions to problems that are as much theirs as ours. The edifice of Moslem civilization, which is old, and has given the West so much of its mathematics, science, medicine, art and literature, is threatened by the fanatics, the terrorists.

In this country, we do not see our rulers consulting moderate Moslems, or if they do, they keep it quiet. And there must be equivalent people in the United States.

Meanwhile it would be a help to stop using the word "terrorist" like a witch's spell, and restrict it to the real terrorists.

"Ignorant armies" like the Taliban are not terrorists. Saddam Hussein is not a terrorist—he is a brutal dictator, on a model we are familiar with: Stalin, Hitler, Pol Pot. Iran is not a terrorist regime, though it may be sheltering terrorists. It is another brutal regime whose human rights record, according to the United Nations, is among the worst.

Terrorists are those highly trained ruthless groups waiting in the United States and the countries of Europe to murder, poison and destroy. Let us catch them, if we can. In order to understand them we must learn the laws that govern cults and brainwashing.

—Doris Lessing

Acknowledgments

This book was originally undertaken because of what I learned at a year-long seminar on new religions organized by Richard Anthony, Ph.D., Jacob Needleman, Ph.D., and Paul Schwartz, Ph.D., of the Center for the Study of New Religious Movements. I am grateful for the rich experience and creative environment they provided.

I am indebted to the many people whose work has provided substance for this book, especially Ben Bagdikian, Irving Janis, and Idries Shah.

A number of persons who read the manuscript or portions of it at various stages of its development made useful comments and suggestions: Walt Anderson, Ph.D.; Enoch Calaway, M.D.; Arthur Colman, M.D.; Etta Deikman; Charles Gompertz, D.D.; Lynn Howard; George Leonard; Mel Morgan; Stuart Miller; Robert Ornstein, Ph.D.; Alan Skolnikoff, M.D.; Frances Vaughn, Ph.D.; Roger Walsh, M.D.; Margaret-Rose Welch; Leighton Whitaker, Ph.D. John Levy was particularly generous with his time and comments.

Joanne Wyckoff, Chris Kochansky, Wendy Strothman, and the late Suzanne Lipsett gave valuable editorial help with the original book. I would also like to thank Fred Hill for helping to bring the earlier work to publication.

I am particularly indebted to David Cole, my publisher and editor, who suggested widening the scope of the earlier book to address terrorism and our response to it. His encouragement, enthusiasm, and fine editorial judgment have made that possible.

Finally, I wish to thank "Hugh" and "Clara" for their courage in telling their story so that others would benefit.

Introduction

THE SEPTEMBER 11 ATTACK on the World Trade Center seemed to fling us bodily into a new world, one in which a multitude of people has as its objective the killing of U.S. citizens and the disruption of society. We are confronted by a group of people—people who have been training and plotting for years—ready to sacrifice themselves in the righteousness of their cause and the surety of paradise as their reward. In some ways this threat is the worst that the United States and other nations have ever experienced. As a consequence the world has changed irrevocably, for everyone, although most people do not appreciate the depth of that change.

What makes the change less obvious is that terrorist actions have been common throughout human history. Even in recent times we have experienced the actions of a Timothy McVeigh blowing up a government building in Oklahoma City under the anti-government ideological influence of the Patriot Militia Movement. Overseas we have the example of the Japanese Aum cult releasing sarin gas in the Tokyo subway, but these seemed, each in its own way, a random act of psychopathology.

With a relatively sophisticated leadership and widespread support in the Middle East, al Qaeda is different. Pursuant to the goal of making Islam the dominant culture of the world, its leaders have indicated their readiness to employ nuclear, chemical, and biological weapons, and there is every indication that this threat will be with us for a long time. Given such a global, hidden, religiously based conspiracy, how should we respond?

In 1990, I wrote *The Wrong Way Home*, an analysis of cult behavior as it manifests in ordinary social, government, business, and professional groupings not usually defined as cults. I focused on four principal cult behaviors: dependence on a leader; compliance with the group; avoiding dissent; and devaluing the outsider. I suggested that the most useful question to pose is not, "Is this group a cult?" but "How much cult behavior is taking place?"

Much of my work as a psychiatrist consists of helping people become aware of the fantasies that influence what they do and how they feel. Interestingly, it is not fantasies of power and riches that cause the most trouble, but those of receiving protection, nurture, comfort, or praise; of someone keeping count, noting deeds, thoughts, and efforts. It doesn't matter who a person is, no matter how outwardly independent, a child's wish for a powerful, protective parent waits in the depths of the psyche and seeks expression. And express itself it does. The result is cult behavior—even in people who do not belong to cults.

Usually the word cult refers to a group led by a charismatic leader with spiritual, therapeutic, or messianic pretensions who indoctrinates members with his or her idiosyncratic beliefs. Typically members are dependent on the group for their emotional and financial needs and have broken off ties with those outside. The more complete the dependency and the more rigid the barriers separating members from nonbelievers, the more danger the cult will exploit and harm its members.

While a number of books have been written about cults, Robert Jay Lifton's landmark study of Chinese brainwashing, *Thought Reform and the Psychology of Totalism*, was perhaps the first to explain the cognitive mechanisms operating in totalistic environments.[1] Lifton shows how extreme cults—where authorities have complete control over people—use their power to convert others to their own rigid set of beliefs. In chapter two I describe a homegrown cult with just such a pattern.

Nevertheless our everyday society is not totalistic. We are not subject to the kind of control exercised by the Chinese communists who held prisoners by force, or to the psychologically coercive environments of the worst cults. However, I believe that behavior and patterns of thought qualitatively similar to these can be found in all of us, despite our living in an open society, uncoerced, free to select our sources of information and our companions. We need to understand the cult behavior that operates unnoticed in everyday life.

Toward the end of his book, Lifton remarked that childhood helplessness and dependency produce "a capacity for totalism." I will focus in detail on the way in which the longing for parents persists into adulthood and results in cult behavior that pervades normal society. When I speak of a wish for parents, I am not speaking of transference—the re-experiencing of a specific parental relationship—but of a yearning for parents in the most general sense. This longing results in fantasies of wise, powerful guardians even in those who are themselves looked up to by others, the best educated, the most cynical. Such fantasies exist in the borderlands of consciousness and may seldom be noticed, but they may be superimposed on people who occupy real positions of authority, success, and power, or their images may be displaced to a heavenly realm. Only by recognizing the indwelling wish can we gain freedom from the childhood world of vertical relationships and gain an eye-level perspective.

Such recognition is not easy. Freud made us aware that childhood experience may be expressed in the malfunctioning of the adult; this developmental understanding is now part of our worldview. But despite our sophistication in matters of individual pathology, we lack sufficient recognition of the dependency wishes that all of us express in covert form.

It is difficult to write convincingly about everyday cult behavior because some of the words I must use may sound like psychiatric jargon: dependency, unconscious fantasies, longings for security. Everyone exempts himself or herself from the description. The psychologically sophisticated are likely to think they are beyond these things, and others may think that only weaklings have such vulnerabilities. To try to circumvent this problem, I will make extensive use of examples drawn from a number of sectors of society: government, large corporations, the media, psychiatry, and religion. Finally, I will address the special area of terrorism and our response to it.

In chapter eight I examine both the al Qaeda organization and our own response to the crisis that confronts us. I show how cult behavior is manifested in al Qaeda and its allied groups and ask some vital questions: Are we manifesting cult thinking in our response to the attack and to the threat of future violence? What do we need to be realistic in dealing with this unprecedented danger? How has the world changed?

In looking at these issues, I try to suggest possible solutions that address the underlying causes.

The price of cult behavior is diminished realism. We cannot afford that now, if we ever could. Fortunately, awareness is a potent antidote. The goal of this book is to increase that awareness.

1 The Cult Mirror

SOME YEARS AGO I TOOK PART in a research seminar on new religious movements, the religious and utopian groups that sprang up in the 1960s and 1970s and made the term "cult" familiar to all newspaper readers.[1] Like everyone else, we in the seminar were impressed by the power of cult groups to dominate their members. A most extreme example was the Peoples Temple of San Francisco, whose mass suicide in Guyana was regarded as a piece of insanity, a horror that could be condemned without hesitation, in part because it appeared so alien to our lives. Other groups were only slightly less notorious for such activities as mass sterilization of their men or prostitution of their women; some cults engaged in the breaking up of families and financially exploited devotees, actions less newsworthy but nonetheless damaging.

In reading about cults, most of us in the seminar felt repulsion and fear, but also fascination. Cults present us with images of surrender, violence, sex, and power. We respond to them with avid interest because they speak to unconscious wishes. Moreover, we can watch at a seemingly safe distance because the cults of which we are aware usually have foreign trappings or unusual social structures that separate them from ordinary society and from ourselves. Without such markings, however, cult behavior is not usually recognized, especially when this behavior is our own.

The seminar research group interviewed former cult members. We talked first with a man and a woman who had escaped from the Peoples Temple camp in Guyana on the morning of the mass suicide. These witnesses were not college graduates, nor were most members of the Peoples Temple. At subsequent meetings we interviewed a married couple who had belonged to quite a different cult, one whose members were highly educated, possessing graduate degrees in psychology or related fields. (They had worked as psychotherapists and teachers, just as we in the seminar did.) After that, people spoke who had been members of a utopian rehabilitation group for ex-convicts, and, still later, we heard from members and ex-members of several other new religions.

The variety of personalities involved, of differing racial, economic, religious, educational, and social backgrounds, was impressive. What was most striking was that no matter whom we interviewed, the stories of involvement in exploitive, harmful cults were similar. A distinct pattern of seduction, coercion, corruption, and regression emerged, no matter what the outward trappings, no matter what dogma or purpose the group espoused. Basic human responses had been elicited by a fundamentally similar process.

A COMMON STORY

At the time they joined their particular cult, most of the people we interviewed had been dissatisfied, distressed, or at a transition point in their lives. Typically, they desired a more spiritual life, a community in which to live cooperatively; they wanted to become enlightened, to find meaning in serving others, or simply to belong. An encounter with an enthusiastic, attractive, friendly person served to introduce each of them to a group whose outer appearance was quite benign. At some point during that introductory phase an intense experience took place which was interpreted as validating the claim that the leader and the group were special, powerful, spiritual; that they could give the person what he or she wanted. This experience might have been an altered state of consciousness (induced by the leader or the group via meditation, chanting, or the laying on of hands), a powerful therapeutic experience, or just a wonderful feeling of being accepted and welcomed—of "coming home."

Won over, the newcomer joined the group, embracing its doctrines and practices. Soon the cult's demands increased and the new member was asked to devote increasing amounts of time, money, and energy to the group's activities. These demands were justified as necessary to fulfill the group's goals; willingness to comply was always interpreted as a measure of the recruit's commitment and sincerity. In order to continue, most did comply, sacrificing much for the sake of the stated high purposes of the group (often put in terms of saving the world).

Relationships outside the group became difficult to maintain. The former life of the new member was given up; contact with outsiders was discouraged and the demands of the new life left little opportunity for extra-group activities. However, the sacrifices were compensated for by the convert's sense of belonging and purpose. The group and the leader (at least initially) gave praise and acceptance.

Gradually, however, an iron fist emerged. Deviation from group dogma brought swift disapproval or outright rejection. The message to the convert became clear: what the group had given the group could take away. In time, he or she submitted to—and participated in—cruel, dishonest, and contradictory practices out of fear of the leader and the group, which by then had become the convert's sole source of self-esteem, comfort, and even financial support. Actions that conflicted with the convert's conscience were rationalized by various formulas provided by the leader. (For example, in one group lying to potential converts was explained as "divine deception" for the good of those deceived.) Critical evaluation of the leader and the group became almost impossible, not only because it was punished severely, but also because the view of reality presented by the cult had no challengers. Discordant information was excluded from the group's world.

Exploitation intensified and the recruit regressed into a fearful submission. Couples might be separated; members would inform on each other. Morals were corrupted and critical thinking suppressed. Often the group's leader deteriorated as well, becoming increasingly grandiose, paranoid, or bizarre. In most cases, paranoid thinking tended to mark the entire cult and reinforced the group's isolation.

Our witnesses told of how, eventually, the demands became unbearable; a mother might be told to give up her child or her husband, or a spouse directed to take a different sexual partner. Although often the person would agree to the new requirement, sometimes he or she would not. In such cases, when the member finally refused to comply with the leader or the group's demands, he or she left precipitously, often assisted by a person outside with whom some contact and trust had been maintained.

Leaving such a group was a flight because the group's reaction was known to be severe and punitive. Apostates were excommunicated. It was not uncommon for ex-converts to fear that they had been damned or had lost their souls as a consequence of leaving the group. (In some cases former members were convinced the group would hunt them down and kill them.) Many went through months of struggle to reestablish their lives, wrestling with the questions: How could I have been involved in such a thing? How could I have done what I did to other members of the group? Were my spiritual longings all false? Who and what can I trust? At the same time, the closeness the group offered was often sorely missed, and until the ex-member's life was reconstituted, he or she wondered at times if leaving the group had been a mistake. This turmoil gradually diminished, but for many a sense of shame for having participated in the cult and a frustrated rage at having been betrayed lingered for a long time.

THE DEPENDENCY FANTASY

After listening to many variants of this story, I began to see that cults form and thrive not because people are crazy, but because they have two kinds of wishes: they want a meaningful life, to serve God or humanity; and they want to be taken care of, to feel protected and secure, to find a home. The first motives may be laudable and constructive, but the latter exert a corrupting effect, enabling cult leaders to elicit behavior directly opposite to the idealistic vision with which members entered the group.

Usually, in psychiatry and psychology, the wish to be taken care of (to find a home, a parent) is called dependency, and this is a rather damning label when applied to adults. Adults are not supposed to be dependent in that way, relying on another as a child would rely on a mother or father. We are supposed to be autonomous, self-sustaining, with the capacity to go it alone. We do recognize that adults need each other for emotional support, for giving and receiving affection, for validation; that is acceptable and sanctioned. But underlying such mature interdependency is the longing of the child, a yearning that is never completely outgrown. This covert dependency—the wish to have parents and the parallel wish to be loved, admired, and sheltered by one's group—continues throughout life in everyone. These wishes generate a hidden fantasy or dream that can transform a leader into a strong, wise, protective parent and a group into a close, accepting family. Within that dream we feel secure.

Who does not recognize the feelings portrayed in the following Peanuts© cartoon?

The wish to ride in the back seat of the car—the dependency dream—has great strength and tenacity. It should be recognized as a permanent part of the human psyche even though in adults it ceases to be as visible as it is in childhood. This dream is dangerous because in its most extreme form it generates cults and makes people vulnerable to exploitation, regression, and even violence. Even in the less intense, less obvious manifestations that occur in everyday society, the dependency dream may impair our ability to think realistically. If we recognize our dependent wishes for what they are we can make appropriate corrections in thought and behavior, but usually we do not.

Rather, we engage in thinking and behavior more subtle than that of the Peoples Temple but qualitatively similar. The back seat of the car does not carry us home.

Eventually, we in the seminar were unable to maintain the belief that cults were something apart from normal society. The people telling us stories of violence, cruelty, and perversion of values were like ourselves. After listening and questioning we realized that we were neither different from nor superior to the ex-cult members, that we were vulnerable to the same dependency wishes, capable of the same betrayals and cruelty in circumstances in which our sense of reality was manipulated.

As I studied the psychological mechanisms that made the cult experience possible, I began to recognize uncomfortably familiar processes. A little reflection provided many specific instances of my own compliance—conscious and unconscious—with the values and preferences of my peers, compliance that I had rationalized or ignored because I preferred to think of myself as very independent. Since no radical change or disruption of my life occurred and I was not acting at the behest of a charismatic leader or occult group, it had not occurred to me that I might be behaving like one who has been captured by a cult. Nevertheless, I now realize that the motivations and manipulations constituting cult behavior are present in varying degrees in my own life and that they play a role in the lives of most of us as they operate in our educational systems, the business world, religion, politics, and international relations. Just as many of the more notorious cults have proven to be costly and destructive, so ordinary cult behavior is damaging and harmful to some degree wherever it occurs, no matter how normal its outward appearance.

When the seminar began I viewed cults as pathological entities alien to my everyday life. By the time it ended, I realized that the dynamics of cult behavior and thinking are so pervasive in normal society that almost all of us might be seen as members of invisible cults. In fact, as I will argue, society can be viewed as an association of informal cults to which everyone belongs. Yet the groups most of us belong to do not appear strange, flamboyant, esoteric, or unnatural, nor do they defy society with lurid and violent behavior. Social infrastructures and behaviors that are similar to those of the Peoples Temple go unnoticed.

Surely, the reader may ask, while it is true that serious consequences result from membership in extreme cults, how can you say harm comes from the groups that make up normal society? I certainly don't recognize such effects in groups to which I belong. I am indeed talking about normal society, in which the damage resulting from cult-like behavior is not as obvious as that headlined in the newspapers. Our own cult story is much less pronounced, with no noticeable beginning and no end; our perceptions, beliefs, and critical judgments are affected nonetheless.

We Americans live in a constitutional democracy, priding ourselves on the freedoms we have achieved. We live, travel, and work without internal passports; we have free choice of job or profession; we may hold any belief and, within wide limits, do anything, say anything, write anything, and protest anything. We choose our governing officials from a list we have ourselves determined.

Democracy is based on an "eye-level" world in which we look directly at each other; every citizen is a peer. Political power is delegated, not inherited, not taken, not given by divine right, but bestowed by each of us. However, I believe that a danger exists even in democracies that the omnipresent authoritarian impulse will manifest itself in disguised form, will lead us toward a world in which we are always looking up at those who must be obeyed or down at those who must obey us. This is so because authoritarianism draws its strength from the same source that supports cult behavior: dependency on groups and leaders.

I believe that we need to bring into awareness the unconscious motivations and excluded information that influence our behavior and thought at the personal, national, and international levels. This requires that we first understand the dynamics of obvious cults and then address similar processes in ourselves and in ordinary society. Such understanding can provide us with tools for detecting cult behavior—our own as well as that of others—and enable us to step outside the cult circle.

I will begin with the history of a group that evolved into an extreme cult. The story is told by two of the group's converts, a real couple who underwent the experiences chronicled, although all the names used in my account are fictional and other changes have been made in their story.

"Hugh and Clara Robinson" were members of the cult for nearly a decade. Their story is significant because what they began in joy ended in terror and pain, their own relationship almost destroyed. The progression from Heaven to Hell was gradual, the steps of the descent justified in the name of God and said to be required if the group was to save the world, as it came to believe it could. The Robinsons' history is also significant because they were an intelligent, well-educated, normal couple—yet they came to believe in evil forces and in a group soul that could hold their own souls captive. Prior to their departure from the cult they and other members were spending as many as sixteen hours a day conducting one another through rites of "cleansing," exorcism, and the warding-off of devils. It may be difficult for the reader to identify with the Robinsons in this final, bizarre phase, but their story is classic and their vulnerability is shared by everyone to a greater extent than we realize.

Hugh and Clara escaped; others have not. Although it is important that we know about cults to avoid being caught in them, it is even more important that we study such groups to become aware of the hidden cult thinking operating unnoticed in our daily lives. Cults are mirrors of ourselves.

2 Hugh and Clara

A CASE HISTORY

WHEN HUGH AND CLARA ROBINSON joined Life Force it was an open, friendly, informal gathering of people who had become interested in the teachings of a charming man, Thomas Correll, a psychologist who lived in England, and whom many of the group had visited. Correll met with whomever wanted to consult him, functioning more like a teacher than a traditional psychotherapist. He had developed a system of philosophy and techniques—life force psychology—designed to bring about psychotherapeutic change and personality growth. The sophistication of the theory, the effectiveness of the techniques, the sweetness and joy emanating from the man and, in particular, his emphasis on the spiritual combined to make Correll, and what he taught, very attractive to the highly educated, psychologically oriented men and women, mostly in their twenties and thirties, who began to meet together to carry on and promote his work.

The Robinsons had first encountered life force psychology when they participated in a workshop led by a very dedicated couple, Alex and Barbara Monroe. During that weekend, Hugh and Clara were guided in individual fantasies that were like dream journeys, and for the Robinsons the results were uplifting beyond their expectations:

CLARA: I had the experience of feeling more loved and accepted than I'd ever felt in my whole life. It was a real downflow of energy within me, just amazing. I had the feeling that this was something that I'd always wanted, that I had been looking outside myself for—and there it was.

HUGH: I had a very deep personal experience, realizing that I wasn't alone, that there were other people who cared about the same things I did. So I felt a brotherhood among these people.

After this experience the Robinsons wanted to learn more. They took several courses of study with the Monroes, traveled abroad to study with Thomas Correll for a few months, and decided to devote themselves full-time to studying and teaching life force psychology.

At that time Clara Robinson was over thirty, married, and the mother of a young child. She had a bachelor's degree in English literature and had completed additional graduate work as well. Clara's relationships with her parents, siblings, and peers had been good. A leader in both high school and college, she was superior in intelligence and socially adept.

Clara's involvement with the Life Force group was rooted in her sense of a special beauty in the world, a transcendent quality. When she was a little girl she spent a lot of time alone in nature. The trees and birds were a special source of delight, as was her perception that "light was very nearby, a feeling of things being very beautiful, in a way that I never found too many people to share it with . . . I had that when my child was born, too: the miracle of life."

Except for one teacher, the first person she met with whom she could share that reality was her husband, Hugh. She remembers thinking, He knows the secret thing, too. This shared sense of a greater reality was a central theme to their relationship. Clara wondered why more people didn't have that feeling of special beauty.

Later, life force psychology provided a way of understanding that experience. For the first time Clara could share her perception with others, could integrate this secret, precious part of herself into her life in a beneficial way. She found a way to express herself and to teach principles and techniques that she believed could help others as well.

The system answered other needs as well. After Clara and Hugh were married, they discovered the human potential movement and Clara joined a therapy group that unleashed a great deal of fear in her. Her anxiety became progressively worse, and psychotherapy did not help. At this point in her life Clara encountered the Monroes and had her initial "transformation session," a profound and exhilarating experience, convincing her that the transformation process—as taught by Alex and Barbara—would provide the help she was seeking.

The experience took place in a group setting. Clara had volunteered to work on her fear; "In those days I would do anything to get help." Alex Monroe asked, "What are you afraid of?"

CLARA: I'm afraid I will float away.

ALEX: Can you see what you are afraid you will float away from?

CLARA: No, but I know what it is—it's myself as a grown woman.

ALEX: Can you see her?

CLARA: And then I saw this really wonderful, grounded Earth Mother . . . like an enormous earthy woman . . . the opposite of my kind of thin, wispy, mystic identification. And I cried and cried and cried. It was just wonderful. And he [Alex] worked with that in dialog and imagery and then he said, "There's a wise old man in the sun" and so I went up toward the sun and there was this wise man and he said to me, "My child," and I climbed in his lap, like a child— he was very much like a father, as I retell it I realize that—I just felt like I was home. I felt a downflow of love and affection that I have never felt before or since . . . like being totally okay. This must be what I have always been looking for . . . "I'm really all right. . . . " . . . It was very important . . . like this big sigh in it . . . I could rest. It was that experience that made me feel that I needed to do more of whatever this system was.

Alex told her she could think of that wise person any time she wanted. Afterward Clara did that and it helped calm her, as did visualizing the earth mother. This vivid experience of what I would interpret as the dependency dream was profoundly important to Clara. "It felt like unconditional love, being totally accepted." She felt it had spiritual connotations as well. Clara thought everyone must want and should have this acceptance.

Hugh was also over thirty when he joined Life Force. He had studied at Princeton and was working on a Ph.D. in psychology. Like Clara, he had good relationships with his family and was close to his father and mother whom he described as spiritual people although not formally religious: "They were just committed to making changes for a better world." His father and mother both worked for liberal causes.

Throughout his school years Hugh had been an outstanding student and leader, yet he felt isolated from his peers. There was an artistic, sensitive side to himself that he was unable to share. Hugh appeared strong, confident, and successful in studies and athletics. He was a musician, popular with women, and the leader of his class. Inside, however, he felt alone, missing the security of his home environment where the spiritual part of himself was shared and supported. He strongly associates this spiritual aspect of his life with his love of music; when asked about early mystical experiences he refers to his artistic side:

> I had this intense, private spiritual life which I had always experienced in terms of music . . . what I would call superconscious experiences . . . and then at age nineteen, in the Rockies in Colorado, I had a spontaneous experience of unity with everything. That never left, in a way. I think that was always a backdrop to my searching.

This sense of the spiritual Hugh felt unable to share with his friends. Looking back, he recognizes that his peers' jealousy of his accomplishments added to his sense of isolation, "so there was this mixture of not feeling really connected but yet being admired by them and being a leader."

In college Hugh had a few good friends but felt even more like a loner. He was disillusioned with the pretensions of academic life and ceased trying to achieve the top.

At the time he encountered Life Force, Hugh was ripe for something to believe in, "to put my energy into. . . . I had a wife and child and I didn't feel too comfortable with what it meant to be in the world and make a living. I was anxious about my life and wasn't sure that it was going to work out. I'd had to leave thing after thing because somehow it didn't satisfy me."

During that first workshop with the Monroes, Alex conducted Hugh in a long fantasy in which he climbed a mountain. At one point Alex suggested that Hugh become a beautiful tree that had been created in the fantasy. He did so.

There was this wonderful flow of energy, of roots and light . . . very powerful. I had never experienced anything like this before.

Alex then suggested that he leave the tree, continue on up the mountain, and then look at the sun.

Out of the sun came this figure and he came down . . . Greek, with a Franciscan robe on . . . a marvelous black beard, sort of green eyes . . . very alive and powerful figure and he just looked at me and we embraced and there was this wonderful feeling between us. Then we threw our arms around each other and we said, "Let's take on the world!" There was this sense that we were going to work together to help the rest of the world.

The guided fantasy went on for about an hour. At the end of it, Hugh opened his eyes. The original group of twenty-five had been reduced to four in addition to Alex and Barbara. It was midnight. Two of those who stayed had met Hugh previously, two had not.

They were all men . . . this was overwhelming to me, it was as powerful as the daydream . . . these people had stayed to be with me during this thing. Here were people who were sticking by me and not abandoning me for not understanding. And then Barbara said to me, "You don't have to be alone anymore." I just wept and wept . . . that I didn't have to be alone anymore.

Hugh and Clara shared an intuitive sense of a larger reality that was very important to them. However, I believe that this perception was confused with unresolved dependency longings that led them to interpret the guided daydream as spiritual and to accept the Monroes as guides or agents in that domain. Their enthusiasm for the new system was also due to its affirmation of their perceptions of the numinous world, perceptions that had not been acceptable to their peers. Suddenly, they found meaning, purpose, and helpful work to do.

The procedures and theoretical system of life force psychology had been put together by Thomas Correll, who had taught the Monroes when they had visited him four years before. Alex and Barbara were Correll's chief disciples, seemingly modeled after him in gentleness and altruism and in the loving attention they paid to those who came to learn and be helped by the system. They were totally dedicated to bringing this wonderful new teaching to others, to the world they believed needed it so badly.

Over the next four years life force psychology became popular, numerous workshops were given, and training sessions were developed for mental health professionals. The Robinsons had many sessions with the Monroes and received personal instruction abroad from Correll, as did almost all those who joined the Life Force group at the initial stage. Soon Clara and Hugh began to lead workshops and training sessions, moving to be near the Monroes so they could be more involved in the work. They felt they had the life they had always wanted. The spiritual values formerly split off from their working lives were now directly expressed and shared with a group of peers to whom they felt connected, people who validated and gave support to each other.

Hugh could now put his leadership abilities to use for a cause he believed in. He was appointed to the executive committee of the Life Force Psychology Center and conducted workshops and training sessions all over the United States. The theory of life force psychology particularly appealed to him.

> I loved the ideas; I loved the system. . . . It felt like the most comprehensive and humane way of looking at people I'd found. I could work with these ideas about human nature that fit with how [I felt] when I played music or studied literature or whatever. . . . There was just a very deep personal connection. It was mental as well as emo-

tional . . . like being on a frontier. There was a tremendous amount of excitement and intellectual stimulation . . .

For Clara also, life force psychology and the Life Force fulfilled important needs and involved her deepest feelings:

CLARA: It really fit with what I valued, what I had always hoped for. I must always have been a closet mystic, I suppose . . . suddenly there was a form [for the spiritual] and there was someone teaching who said you can work with people this way. So I gradually got more involved in teaching, in designing workshops. I was doing work with women at that time and there was quite a lot of freedom in the beginning to do my own thing. The workshops were attended and they grew and my confidence in teaching grew.

The members of the Life Force Psychology Center supported and encouraged her teaching.

What was exciting for me was that there was a place for my spiritual experience within the psychological system and I could learn to work with people to evoke that, and have them trust that and tap into it . . . learning how to help people get in touch with more love and compassion and with their creativity. I think affirming is the best word I could use. It just felt like it was affirming the best in people.

Gradually, this sense of high purpose gave rise to feelings of specialness that later led to the devaluation of those outside the group and to the elevation of Alex.

CLARA: [During these early years] there was a growing sense that this group was special and that we were doing something special that nobody else was . . . and that Alex was special.

The Robinsons were happy with their teaching role in Life Force. Five satisfying years went by. They conducted therapy sessions and taught workshops and classes. They believed that what they were doing was making a unique contribution to the world. Hugh in particular felt this to be a time of growth and personal fulfillment. He was an executive of the Center and, at the same time, had good friends in other professional organizations devoted to humanistic and spiritual concerns. He helped plan conferences, gave major presentations, traveled widely, and interacted with Life Force groups in other countries. Thus, for a long time there was a balance between Hugh's involvement with the Life Force Psychology Center and the rest of the world of humanistic and transpersonal psychology.

Clara engaged in similar activities, although to a lesser extent. She divided her life between Center work and her family. While Life Force took up a large part of her time and energy, she felt a reasonable share remained for her son and Hugh. Clara and Hugh were both pleased with the way their lives were going, convinced that Life Force was making a unique and vital contribution to the world.

Then the Center moved to better offices in the city and expanded teaching activities in other parts of the country and to Europe. With that move, the Robinsons' life and that of the others in the group became more and more conflicted, painful, and distorted. More time was demanded from each member. This demand was made by Alex Monroe at a meeting of the executive committee, which transmitted it to a larger meeting that included the other members of the group (such as Clara). Pressure for compliance with this and other demands was usually from the group as a whole although Alex would personally exert extra pressure, if needed, on a balky member.

Clara experienced most of her conflicts with the Life Force group over the issue of commitment to her family. There was a competition for time and energy between the group and her son.

> I dragged my heels [against an increased commitment to the group]. . . . There was a meeting where we were all supposed to make a commitment to take the work of the Center further. I was the last to, as they put it, "put my sword on the table." I said, "I'm not sure I can do it, I'm not sure it's really right for me."

Finally Clara agreed. Such conflicts were continual, but she told herself that giving increasing time to the Center was right because it was needed.

Everyone around me seems to think it's okay . . . all these reasons.
Somehow I let it be all right, I told myself it was all right, even though
I didn't feel good about it. There were lots of things like that. The
first impulse would be, this isn't right. And then someone questions
it . . . maybe it's me or maybe it's someone else . . . and they get really
put down. Sometimes there would be an awful silence in the room,
sometimes it could be twenty people all looking at you incredulously
and someone saying, "How could you worry about that? Don't you
see that we really need to. . . ." There wasn't any opening for a different point of view; there was no space for other opinions. . . . I
told myself it must be right, but I don't think I ever stopped hearing that voice, saying it was not right.

Thus the group enforced compliance and dissent was stifled. Over
the next few years, questionable practices, introduced by Alex, gradually increased, requiring further suppression of the members' sense of
what was right. One such incident concerned a publicity write-up for
Clara's workshops.

There was a real effort to puff up the write-ups [make them look
more impressive]. . . . I had taught several night courses at the university but they wanted to put down that I had taught at the university itself. I remember questioning it and when you would question, from all sides there would come, "Why were you thinking that?
This is an opportunity to get our work more known. . . ." There
would be a response that made me feel like I couldn't keep pushing
for it. I backed down a lot . . . "Clara! How could you suggest that!"
was the message. Alex would say, "Here we are doing such important work and you let that bother you? What a petty little thing to
be concerned with."

A great deal of "psychotherapeutic processing" among Center members took place over the telephone. When the issue was taping phone
conversations, Alex (as always) had many justifications.

CLARA: Incredible, elaborate reasons, sometimes reasons you just
couldn't understand, they were so complicated. The idea was that if

we have a record of phone calls between people if something goes wrong we can have a record and then look and see whose fault it was or what the problem was . . . [As far as outside phone calls were concerned,] Well, by then the outside world was the enemy and so we wanted to know exactly what happened.

Eventually, Alex asked them to tape everything.

CLARA: I really encountered my ability to rationalize. If I had paid attention to all those occasions when everything inside of me said, "No, this isn't right," I couldn't have stayed there. If I had really taken a stand, let's say on the taping, and said, "I will not go along with this," first of all, it would have taken a kind of strength that I don't know I had at the time because everyone in the room [would be saying] "Clara, you want to have dinner with your son? You're so selfish . . ." I would have had to be willing to stand there and have everyone in the room say, "No."

Thus, the group enforced compliance by the use of rhetoric that exploited Clara's idealism for the group's own purposes. Alex led the way. If he was opposed on grounds of principle, Alex attacked those principles by equating them with selfish desires. The members had doubts about Alex's reasoning, but they never really discussed the matter among themselves out of fear that Alex might learn of it. Sometimes, after a meeting, members would walk home together and say, "God, that was weird, wasn't it?"

CLARA: We would sneak those little things to each other. But you could never be sure that that person wouldn't get home and call Alex and say, "Boy, Clara Robinson was really identifying with her desire nature. You should have heard what Clara said after the meeting."

This suspicion extended to close friends.

I couldn't even be sure that Hugh wouldn't do that; I did that on him. There was no safe person to trust with that intuitive sense [of something being wrong]. . . . You couldn't be sure . . . sometimes someone else would say, "Yeah, I didn't like that, either," but you didn't know if that would be kept in confidence. There was no one but your-self to corroborate. If someone coming home had said . . . if we had said together, "It isn't right, what happened to so-and-so . . ." Any of that would have made a tremendous difference—there was none.

So dissent was silenced. Typically, Alex did not demand that mem-bers inform on each other; rather, they were asked to provide infor-mation that could be used to "help" the other person.

CLARA: It used to be a way of getting in with Alex. He was always glad for that information. I remember the first time I was asked to give [information] . . . Alex said, "I'm going to bring this thing up about Jerry and if you could share that piece in the meeting that would be very helpful." I remember [saying] "I'm not sure that is right," but then the rationale would be that it would really help Jerry and I'd say, "Oh, that's right, Jerry can learn from that if he can see that; that will really help him." A lot of things went under that rea-soning—a lot of bad things. Then there were times when people would volunteer . . . getting Alex's favor was a pretty important thing, particularly toward the end, getting his approval. . . . He definitely had real favorites and they'd change. It was never a very secure favoritism; you could lose it at any point.

Hugh's experience was similar. Like the others, he wished for Alex's approval, and fear of losing it led him to compromise his principles and avoid dissent.

HUGH: There were things that were beginning to happen there that I was uncomfortable about. But because my personal connection had been so deep, I kept saying, "It's worth it. This work is so good, it's so effective, that I'll overlook. . . ." Alex lied. Just little things, like changing the date on a letter, but I hated that. And I would say, "Why do we have to do that?" and he would have some quick answer that would say why it was necessary, because someone would screw him if he didn't, basically. And so I said, "Okay. . . ." And then it was lying to people about different situations [in order to control them]. The executive committee would get together and plan exactly what was going to go in the meeting, what was going to happen, so that there was no trust of the natural caring or power or whatever in people in the Center. But because the work was so "good," you know, I loved it, I turned a blind eye. Every year, I'd think, "Something's not right here. And yet, something is so right here." We pushed away a lot of stuff . . . that's what we realize, now, but we didn't at the time.

Alex's power derived from the assumption that he knew much more than the others about the teaching and thus was entitled to special authority. Indeed, it turned out that there had been a secret, mystical side to Thomas Correll that only some knew about, a deep involvement in an esoteric group devoted to occult writings. Correll had given occult books to Alex, who eventually began to teach his own version of the elaborate esoteric system to an inner circle at the Center, those people whom he felt to be most committed to the work.

HUGH: I thought Alex was smarter than me, more evolved, because he knew all this occult stuff . . . [he would] use chapter and verse to rationalize these things. It was like a priest using a Bible. He read it much more than anyone else and no one could refute it.

Thomas Correll died. The Robinsons later recalled that Alex had begun making disparaging comments about Correll prior to the man's death, remarking that he was too vague, too lax, too generous with his time, too indiscriminate, not focused enough, something of a fuddy-duddy. After Correll's death, such comments were more frequent. Alex became the only source of the teaching, the one who determined whether others would or would not continue to receive its benefits. Barbara Monroe became more and more subordinate. As Alex gradually exerted more and more control over the group's other members, their dependence on him increased. While he claimed to work and share power with the executive committee, in fact he subtly retained all power and control in his own hands. The committee soon realized that their job was to discuss and debate until they reached the decision Alex wanted. Alex did not acknowledge what he was doing and maintained the facade of democracy for a long time after it had become perfectly obvious to the others that he was the sole authority.

Clara's request for enough time to be with her child was labeled a selfish desire by the group. She recalls that there had never been any respect for her role as a mother. There was constant pressure on her to comply with the group's demand for more and more time. First, it was all mornings and then it was mornings and two afternoons, then five, and then meetings on Saturday as well.

> CLARA: "Clara, when you really get it that your family is the whole world then you'll understand that David is just one of the many children you are responsible for." When we were asked to take the Center another step, I dragged my heels. There was this noise in my head: "Should I do this? Shouldn't I do this? Maybe it will be wrong and then what?" I remember at one point saying, "I'll do it," and everything got quiet around me and the noise in my head stopped and I thought, "God, maybe that is right. What I am being asked to do is to make a fuller commitment to this good work. . . ." And inside me I thought the quiet or sense of rightness means I'm doing the right thing to get more involved.

After several months of commuting to the new Center, the Robinsons moved to the city. The pressure on group members to give totally of their time and energy became overwhelming.

> HUGH: By that time we were working six or seven days a week . . . leaving at six o'clock in the morning and coming back whenever. We had two cars and sometimes we had to drive separately . . . what that did was to fragment our family life.

Hugh was having a harder and harder time maintaining balance in his professional life as well. His involvements outside the Center drew increasing fire from Alex and the inner circle. He had never been one of Alex's favorites. On the few occasions when Alex had tried to use him as a confidant to help deal with another member, Hugh had felt very uncomfortable and failed the task. On occasions when Hugh disagreed, Alex justified everything with arguments and by citing the occult books. Hugh's rebellions against Alex's control were always short-lived.

HUGH: I would kick up a fuss and then I would give in, that's the pattern. "All for the good" . . . he would get me on the "good." "Oh, I see, for that reason, because it's spiritually right." There was always a host of reasons that would evoke my caring for the cause and then I'd go along with it rather than saying, "Look! The cause is being violated right here!"

When Hugh asserted the importance of his family's needs, Alex would say, "Hugh, if your family was starving and you had one pound of wheat, would you make bread for your family or would you plant it to feed the starving million?"

This appeal to higher purpose, to the greater good, was Alex's stock in trade, and was copied by the group when it needed to pressure uncooperative members.

HUGH: It didn't quite fit but I had to go along with it because intellectually it made sense. I would discount my strong feelings. Everything was to be sacrificed to the greater, the larger: bringing Life Force into people's lives . . . I never won a battle; it was just a matter of how long I could stand up to it before it became too painful and then I would let myself be persuaded and would give in. [But] then I would subvert the system by just going right out and doing what I was doing.

The executive committee attacked Hugh's outside activities.

This allegation of evil began to come at me . . . that I was identified with my "elemental" [selfish nature] and so forth. . . . More and more it would be that I had done something wrong and I had to fix it and I would try. Every time I would return from a committee meeting [of an outside organization] to the Executive Committee of the Center, I was called on the carpet for doing power trips, for not telling them everything that happened, for not getting Alex on the [conference] program. So I felt increasingly at odds but I was confused and wanted to do the right thing. . . . [I was] torn between my loyalties . . . torn to pieces.

Alex planned to establish a graduate school of life force psychology with branches in North and South America and in Europe. It was a very ambitious project and required even more time and effort from group members. The actual establishment of the first of these graduate schools in the city, after the group moved there, was a pivotal event, one which inspired a further intensification of the cult process. Anyone who questioned the direction of the group was seen as an enemy who needed to be controlled or pushed down, whether the questioner was a group member or an outsider. As a result, members became more and more isolated from colleagues in other human service organizations and their time and energy were even more tightly controlled.

Abruptly, Hugh was removed from his position on the executive committee. At a meeting of that body he was told he was not contributing to the "group mind," asked to leave the executive committee's circle, and discontinue almost all activities at the graduate school, where he had been teaching. He was instead given the lowest, least important assignments and asked to teach beginning workshops. Much of his time was spent cataloging cassette tapes and xeroxing. Occasionally, when he was allowed to teach a course at the graduate school, his proposal would be severely criticized.

> I became increasingly filled with fear and self-doubt . . . fear of what the group could do to me, fear of hurt, of rejection; fear of somehow being alone again. I was very alone and had lost whatever fellowship I had in the earlier years that had drawn me toward the group . . . turned against by people within the executive group that I cared about.

At the same time, Clara's loyalties were being drawn away from Hugh toward the group. Lewis, Hugh's close friend, was echoing the group's abuse. Hugh was afraid of being abandoned completely. The isolation he thought he had left behind by joining Life Force now had reappeared within it.

> I was afraid of being alone, afraid of being cast out of Eden . . . even though Eden had turned into Hell . . . afraid of being cast out even farther. There was still, "Well, we're doing the graduate school, Hugh, and you can't think, so you can do these other things and we'll still

be nice to you and we won't tell other people that you are no longer an executive." In other words, there was still "caring" for me and I was still grasping for any care I could get.

For Clara, also, Eden was turning into Hell. Not only did she experience an increasingly painful struggle to meet her son's needs, but her relationship with Hugh came under attack. One evening, late at night, she was called to meet with several executive committee members with whom she had warm ties. They told her that Hugh was having trouble and that they were having trouble with him:

CLARA: Hugh has been asked not to be on the executive committee and we just want you to know that we really value you . . . we want you to stay no matter what happens . . . we want you to know that we really trust what you do.

Lewis offered further reassurance.

LEWIS: Clara, if anything happens, you can come to my house and bring your kid.

CLARA: That always happened whenever anything was done to a couple; the other member of the couple would get a lot of attention: "You're different . . . you're special," whatever . . .

These men whom I cared about made a real effort to get me to stand with them in their condemnation of him [Hugh] and to see him with their eyes. I betrayed our bond in that time . . . there was always truth [in the accusations], there were seeds of truth . . . there was stuff in me that both wanted to hear and also saw some of the things they were saying. And that part of me that was always dependent on Hugh was delighted to get that much attention from these men in the group, just delighted . . . and support for my teaching and all that came after that time. . . . That was just one of those times that I betrayed Hugh and betrayed the bond we had from all those years together.

The meeting with these men had been carefully planned by Alex, and he had met with them earlier to lay out the strategy they were to use on Clara.

The splitting of couples was one of the most malignant and prominent features of Alex's tyranny, the foundation whereby he established and increased his control over the members of Life Force. The support and reality testing provided a given member by his or her trusted partner was subverted; ties and loyalty that supported his or her sense of self-worth were compromised. The guilt experienced may have provided substance to charges later on that the couple harbored evil forces, accusations hurled at them by Alex, the person orchestrating their mutual betrayal.

This direct attempt to split the Robinsons capitalized on the erosion that had already taken place in their relationship. Ever increasing demands on their time left almost no opportunity for them to be together. "Circles of silence," the structure of secrecy that Alex established, further weakened their relationship. The executive committee did not share what happened at their meetings with the senior members, those at the next level down. They, in turn, withheld information from those below them, the members, who did not share with the students. Finally, in the year before the graduate school opened, Hugh and the other executive committee members were asked to take a formal vow of secrecy. Hugh was not to confide in Clara, as he had been doing. As he had done with similar matters in the past, Hugh protested, struggled, but then yielded to the pressure. When he was thrown off the executive committee he was not able to share what had happened with his wife, nor did she confide in him about what had been said to her.

A few months went by before Clara also found herself in trouble. She was said to have "bad energy." This time it was Hugh who was asked to cooperate with the group in dealing with her. When he went out of town to teach they persuaded him to leave Clara a note saying that he wouldn't have any contact with her during the ten days that he would be away. Soon after, they put Clara in "quarantine."

Quarantine was a procedure of restricting a member to his or her house or apartment, having contact with no one except Alex or one other executive that Alex might designate. Quarantined members were supposed to reflect upon their "bad energy" or "power trips" or their "elemental" (basic evil)—Alex had detected. They waited until a phone call came, which might mean being "processed" for hours by Alex or an executive until they saw the error of their ways.

> HUGH: I remember waiting fourteen hours for a phone call in total panic, and it turned out the executive committee had decided not to call me and had gone to bed . . . and I was sitting there, waiting.

The period of quarantine was one of acute deprivation lasting days or months. To an outsider, there would seem to be no reason for a member to put up with it. To understand, one must recognize that despite the negative aspects of Life Force, there were also times when the members laughed together, when the entire group was close and caring, times when they shared food and felt a love for each other that seemed genuine and precious. In quarantine, all this was withdrawn.

> HUGH: People who a day before you had been laughing with, having fun with, working with, would just turn their eyes away; they wouldn't even make eye contact. If you have the experience of love and then you're cut off from it, there's a tremendous motivation to get back to it, tremendous desire to reconnect with that love. . . . And you'll do anything to get back because it makes you feel good . . . makes you feel you're a good person.

The effort to split the Robinsons continued. When Clara fell from grace, Hugh was exhorted to stand up to her, to "be a man!" Hugh later recalled a particular moment when Alex said, "Hugh, we want you to own your power."

> HUGH: For just a minute I had a perception of Hell . . . I saw a devil's face . . . red, everything. It was a perception that the totally opposite thing was happening than what he was saying. I saw that this was Hell . . . and then it [the perception] went again. I rationalized and said, "He wants me to own my power so I am going to go stand up to Clara." I couldn't. I came back from England—she'd been isolated ten days—she met me at the door . . . she was in tears. I came and sat with her and we had a good talk. . . . [later] I told Alex and the others that we'd talked and I got lambasted for giving in, for being

manipulated by her tears. [They said] that I should have been tough and told her to cut out the bullshit. Well, I didn't.

Following the establishment of the graduate school, Alex had placed more and more stress on "the elemental," which he defined as evil, selfishness, the opposite of spirituality, the anti-Christ. This concept came from the esoteric system the group had studied, but Alex magnified it until protecting the group from evil—from within and without—became the major focus of the group's activities. Members who opposed him were said to be yielding to their selfish side, identifying with it, harming the group and themselves through its influence. Although not directly stated, the implied message was that the only hope to free themselves from their own evil lay in Alex's guidance. As Clara recalled, the message was, If you don't watch out, if you don't look, if you don't see evil, if you don't listen to me, you will be caught in eternal Hell.

The ultimate in devaluation was directed against anyone who left the group. They were declared to have completely given in to their elemental, their selfishness, their badness; and whatever had been good in them, their soul itself, was said to have been left behind in the group. Such people were shunned as contaminating forces, and they were declared to have turned against their own souls.

> CLARA: Once you left, they didn't speak to you again. They passed you on the street without speaking, even though you'd been with them for years. . . . There was a feeling toward the end that you ought to be careful of who you got involved with, because you could lose anyone at any minute. Someone you really loved might just go or . . . get bad, so don't get too involved. Anyone you saw as good might flip [become bad] any day . . . your husband, your best friend . . . that's a strange feeling.

Alex was feared because he could judge someone to be bad and the rest of the group would go along. Dissent was invariably punished.

> CLARA: When he would say, "Mary is selfish," we could usually pick out things that would support that. Your seeing would be affected by

it: "Oh yeah! I remember when I had lunch with her last week. . . ." And you'd take an incident that in another setting you might not notice, but you could pull them out . . . particularly if you wanted to get in with him at that moment, you would look for those times. You'd certainly not say, "I haven't seen that; that hasn't been my experience." Boy! If you disagreed with how Alex was seeing it you were in deep trouble. The times I did were invariably used against me, if not at the moment, then later.

Opposition of any kind would call forth processing so that the member could see that he or she had been giving in to their selfish nature Such experiences could be devastating:

CLARA: I had two experiences of being in a large group where I was on the spot for supposedly not being a good person, with about eighteen people—my "friends"—bringing up information about why I wasn't a good person. I don't think I've ever been through anything so awful in my life, but I bought it . . . I think that in some funny way those meetings were usually triggered by a time when a person was seeing that something was wrong . . . being "difficult. . . ." When Alex said, "We're going to have three . . . campuses, continue the Journal of Life Force Psychology and start a training program to compete [with independent Life Force groups in other cities] . . . ," I said, "How can we possibly do this?" My question was met with stony silence from the whole group. Erica worked with me three or four hours the next day to let me see that that was my elemental that had asked that question—not just my common sense!

Coupled with the emphasis on evil was Alex Monroe's growing interest and belief in past lives, a theory of reincarnation at the group level. Alex told the executive committee that they had all been together in many past lives and he had them play out past-life scenarios. One of the first past lives was called the Persian Past Life. Alex was a priest in ancient Persia; Hugh was a king and there was a church-state conflict. Everyone had a part. Typically, Alex did not need to specify the others' roles. Patricia, another member (whom Hugh had been trying to protect from criticism by the executive committee) became his sister.

The priest, Alex, burned Patricia at the stake; thus the group fantasy translated events happening within the group into terms of past lives.

Alex's control over the Life Force members' lives increased further. Each day they were supposed to fill out time sheets detailing every activity conducted throughout the day. Although most hated this, the procedure was rationalized as improving efficiency and it soon became an instrument of control. The sheets were often collected and looked over when a member was thought to be a problem; then there would be a meeting with one or more of the executive committee who would take the errant person to task. Meeting with people outside the group required the permission of the executive committee. Behind them, controlling everything, was Alex.

Supporting Alex's power, keeping the members committed to the organization, no matter how bizarre their lives became, was the shared belief that they were a special group, doing work of great importance to the world.

> CLARA: I think in the end, [we believed that] we were the only people doing this . . . and I remember thinking, "Isn't this strange that [our little group] sitting around could be this special group." I think we had the feeling that Alex was an important articulator of the Christ or the coming of the Christ. . . . I think he believed that more and more himself.

Hugh's behavior continued to be "bad" and he was placed under surveillance. When he went to Baltimore to conduct a workshop, Margaret, one of the executive committee, accompanied and supervised him. Hugh's mother and father lived in Baltimore, but he was not allowed to stay with them. Instead, he checked into a motel. When he did visit his parents, Margaret went with him.

Hugh's brother was involved in the Baltimore Life Force group and a few months after Hugh's visit there trouble developed.

> HUGH: Alex used his power to split up the Baltimore group and my brother became the evil one there. Alex got three of the people to put him and a friend out in twenty-four hours . . . telling them they

couldn't come to their office . . . a kind of strong arm job which was tremendously upsetting to my brother because his friends with whom he had built this thing turned against him. My mother got very upset, understandably, and called up one of her friends [in the Center] who she knew and said, "What is going on there?"

As far as Alex was concerned, this intervention by Hugh's mother made her a source of evil.

HUGH: I went to lunch with Alex and some of the other executives and he said that evil energy was coming from my mother toward the group so I was going to have to cut off from her. I remember feeling this terror because I had seen this happen in other situations and I said, "Oh, my God, it's coming here." But again, I was immobilized, filled with fear and self-doubt, afraid to resist. We did a long session that afternoon, I connected with the Christ . . . Alex used the thing of . . . Christ says, "You have to leave your father and your mother in order to follow me. . . ." I bought it and although I again had this terribly ambivalent feeling of disorientation and confusion and being in over my head, yet, at the same time being too afraid to disagree and, so, I felt I had to go along with it.

Hugh wrote to his parents expressing anger at them for criticizing the organization, telling them that what happened in Baltimore had nothing to do with his group. His parents wrote back letters of apology which Alex read. For a moment, Alex was moved by the letters and admitted that they were very beautiful. Then, a half-hour later, he declared the letters were "too perfect." Hugh was ordered to "cut" from his mother as well as from his brother. This demand was made despite the fact that during that period, Hugh's brother was ill, diagnosed as having cancer. What had been oppressive control by the group and Alex was becoming horrific.

The horror can best be sensed by visualizing the procedure of "cutting," which was practiced more and more in the later phase of the group. Cutting was a process in which members separated themselves from whomever had been declared a source of evil energy—a friend, lover, parent, husband, or wife. They were to visualize cords stretching from their heart to the heart of the other person. Then they were instructed to cut the cords. Sometimes they would go a step further and "burn the image," visualizing the person being consumed by flames. Later, when Clara reflected on all that happened, the cutting she had done was one of the things that was still painful, about which she felt most ashamed.

> I feel I betrayed myself at these times, I let myself do that . . . on some level it didn't seem right, it felt wrong. . . . We asked about it, "Why was this necessary?" Alex would say, "Well, it's not really them that you're burning, it's your projection of them." I feel sad that I did that . . . that one feels really hard to live with.

Hugh discontinued all communication with his parents. His brother became more and more ill, but phone calls from the brother went unanswered. During this time Clara was increasingly critical of Hugh, seeing him as identified with his elemental, accepting Alex's evaluation of him and believing, with the group, that his refusal to speak to his family was correct, although difficult. The rest of the group also supported his action and rewarded him with positive attention.

> HUGH: I got a lot of reinforcement from it which reinforced my desire to get back into the group . . . here were these people approving of me cutting off my parents. . . . But there was a lot of dread and not wanting to go on, [not knowing] how we could get out of this nightmare. But I didn't know how to get out short of leaving and that didn't cross my mind. I guess by that time I knew that if I left I would have lost Clara and David [their son].

Hugh's sister visited him and told him that their brother was worse and that his parents were desperately trying to get through to him, calling the Center repeatedly, but being put off. Hugh called Debbie, one of Alex's inner circle, and told her something must be done. It was agreed that Hugh would phone his brother but that the call would be taped and monitored by Alex and Debbie.

> HUGH: Strangely enough, in the middle of all this chaos, my brother and I sort of reached through to this place of connection between

the two of us . . . talking about his dying, how much we loved each other, how we cared . . . and I have this tape which I listen to every once in a while.

About a week later, Alex worked on Clara to convince her to tell Hugh to leave their house.

CLARA: Alex said Hugh's energy continued to be bad and I, too, felt that he [Hugh] didn't seem good . . . and then, after a meeting, with about ten other people watching . . . Alex talked with me to the point of my deciding what was really best for Hugh was for me to ask him to leave the house . . . and I cried and cried and cried . . . it was very hard.

As soon as Clara agreed to tell Hugh to leave, something happened to her that seemed to validate the decision.

When I made that choice, I had a lot of energy coming in, I mean literally . . . not only did everyone in the room say, "Clara, you're so brave and I really support this and I see how hard it is," but something happened in my head . . . I felt sort of strong and full . . . I saw this happen to Mary . . . when she chose to leave Bill, to stay in the group and let Bill quit . . . the same kind of downflow happened . . . it is like some letting go and you get more energy . . .

I interpreted it inwardly, "Oh, not only do they say it is all right but look what is happening to me!" I saw that again and again . . . for instance when Margaret announced she was leaving Fred, when Dick announced he was divorcing Connie and was never going to see Connie and his children again—that has got to be one of the worst stories in the whole group . . . all those times those people looked big and shiny . . . Margaret when she said, "I'm not going to be with Fred," looked as beautiful as I had ever seen her and inside of me I went, "God, it must be right—look at her!"

Probably, what Clara and other members in such situations experienced was the effect of a sudden release from the intense conflict that was tearing at them, coupled with a child-like surrender, a letting go to the protection and power of the parent/family group. Later on, when he or she had finally left Life Force, the reality of what had been done became clear.

Clara experienced this letting-go phenomenon again when, a short time later, she was asked to break off communication with her own mother.

> I know this second hand. They said one night, "Clara has got to leave her mother"—that came up around the dinner table—so they called me down. . . . They worked on me and worked on me and I just wouldn't budge on it. And Alex said, "Clara, I think you're asking Hugh to do something you're not willing to do." That was heavy and I realized that was probably true . . . and then he had me go up [in imagery] . . . there was a star we used to see and he said, "Ask the star what to do." Then, somehow, the star said something about "You need to let go of your mother and follow me," . . . or something like that. What happened was that again I got that really big hit of right- ness . . . I cried and then, "Oh, that's right, I do need to do that." I remember at that moment Alex was saying, "If you do that, He [Christ] can take care of her too, help her more." And I said, "Oh, that's right." At that moment I thought I was loving her and that he [Alex] was, too.

Clara had her phone disconnected and changed her number so that her mother could no longer reach her. Her very perception of her mother was altered.

> When I was out of touch with my mother I would get letters from her. I would read them in the set [context] that she—or part of her— was trying to get me away from this work, trying to get me off my spiritual path. When you read a letter with that in your head it almost feels like there's [negative] energy in the letter. It's amazing because I've also seen those letters later, when it wasn't like that at all.

A week after Hugh made his last phone call to his dying brother, Clara told him to leave the house. He packed his bags and spent the night in a motel.

> HUGH: It was the worst night of my life. I felt like I had lost every- thing. There was no Clara and David, no contact with group mem-

bers, any family members. My only contact was with Alex and Debbie. I was totally surrounded in darkness. I did come through that night realizing two things: that light was important, spiritual light . . . and that giving was important.

A few weeks later, Hugh's brother died. His family had been send-ing telegrams as his condition worsened but Clara, having been told that Hugh did not want to see them, passed them on to the executive committee.

HUGH: By then, they had influenced her very much. I certainly felt betrayed by her, too. So my brother died and I didn't know when . . . that was one request I made to Alex and Debbie: that I would know the day he died. They wouldn't tell me because they said I was holding on to my brother. I found out that he had died a week or so after when my sister was threatening to come find me. So the executive committee had to do something, had to tell me. Otherwise, I don't think they would have.

Hugh continued in quarantine, having contact only with the exec-utive committee. Several months after Clara asked him to leave the house, the group began pressing her to file for a divorce. She resisted, but eventually agreed and wrote to Hugh informing him of her deci-sion. When she told her son David of the plan he became very upset, screamed, pounded on the floor and then ran out of the house. When he finally returned he phoned Alex's children, who were his friends. This created a disturbance in the Monroe household, with the result that Alex's wife Barbara had to be processed.

Alex had no sympathy for David's distress and interpreted his behav-ior as showing that David was elemental, that he was using his pain at his parents' separation to manipulate people. It was a theory of Alex's that when a child is born the mother sees the evil part of the baby but does not want to recognize it. He said that it was very important that the mother, in this case, Clara, be aware of the evil element in her child and teach him not to act on it. Alex told Clara to go to a special room at the Center where she could scream, pound pillows, and express rage at David, while he [Alex] guided the experience over the telephone. As standard procedure, a team of group members gathered in another location to support the processing by engaging in "subjective work," "cleaning up" Clara from contaminating influences.

> CLARA: [They would be saying,] "Well, I see Clara connected with David, so let's cut Clara from David and let's burn David's image. Oh, and Clara is connected with Lewis, too, and Hugh. Let's clean her up (cut her from them).

Throughout the session, Alex kept insisting that Clara see the evil part in David.

> CLARA: I remember saying, "I don't want to see this, I don't want to see this." And Alex saying, tenderly, "Clara, it's all right, it's all right. He's just a boy trying to find his way." And I thought, "Oh, that's right." And, "You can help him, you can help him with it [the evil part] if you let yourself see it." I believed it for a few days . . . and Alex would tell me that I really needed to discipline David . . . there was a lot of stuff about David's evil part . . . it really pushed me to my limit.

After Hugh received Clara's letter asking for a divorce, he wrote back that he still wanted responsibility for his son, whom he hadn't seen in four months. He gave the letter to the executive committee, who kept it and did not give it to Clara.

> CLARA: We came to fear and distrust each other. Hugh was afraid I was this awful way, and I was afraid he was the way Alex was telling me.
>
> HUGH: We were taught to see the other as evil. Everybody began to see everybody else as predominantly this evil part, the part that was selfish and wanted to control people, that was separative, and so forth.

At this stage, to leave the group was a fearsome step because it meant, literally, to be damned.

> HUGH: Increasingly, one's spiritual fate became identified with the group. So we all thought our souls were members of this group soul and that if you got taken over by your evil part you would be cut off

from your soul. "This is the way to salvation and if you deviate in any way, you're siding with your evil part, you're identifying with it, you're making it bigger." If you thought about leaving the group you had to face the fact that in that system you'd be spiritually damned.

Members came to believe that without the help of Alex Monroe and the Life Force group, a person would have no chance of avoiding "the left-hand path," their evil side would overcome them despite their best intentions.

CLARA: It was never really said, but that was the implication . . . to leave meant to be eternally lost or caught, trapped in the selfish, comfort-seeking part of you that didn't care about the larger world, about alleviating suffering. We began to talk about it more and more and people who left were seen that way, "Poor Jennie, she just went to her selfishness." When we finally left that was the fear we had to struggle with.

Nevertheless, Clara did manage to leave the group, just three days before she was to start divorce proceedings against Hugh. At the time, she had been in quarantine again.

First when Hugh was in quarantine I was very much in favor and getting lots of attention . . . then I lost favor . . . I began to be seen as bad by Alex and a number of other people. One of them was Mary, a close friend. She turned me in to Alex and that was really the final straw . . .
    If Mary is going to see me this way, who else is there? I'm not with my husband; I'm out of contact with my parents; I'm making my son bad . . . and now Mary thinks I'm bad.

One morning Clara was told that the executive committee had some subjective work for her to do. For the first time, Clara refused. She was immediately told to cut from Lewis and Hal (who both had recently left the group) and two or three other members who were thought to be influencing her.

CLARA: I don't know if I even did it but I said that I need to take the day off. . . . So I walked all day long and around where Hugh was liv-

ing hoping I would run into him. I think that was the day that I began
to consider going and to let that thought be a reality. The fact that
Lewis and Hal had left already really influenced me. Leaving became
an option in that universe, it suddenly became a possibility . . . something you could do . . . leaving exists . . . it was real . . . and it hadn't
been up 'til then.

For Clara, the deciding issue was her son.

I sometimes thought . . . [what enabled me to leave] was the mother
lion energy in me. It was like . . . "My husband, my parents and my
friends, but not my baby . . . you just can't have him. I don't care if
you're right about this, I'm not going to let you have him." . . . And
that got me out of there as much as anything did. Alex was capturing every piece of my life, every relationship I had, every piece of
my time . . . Oh, God! . . . capturing it and taking it into himself.
I'm glad I had a child, that was the touchstone, although in the week
before I left there was one moment when I considered I would give
him up if Alex asked me to. . . . I remember that thought coming
into my head, "Am I really committed here? Would I give up my
son if I was asked to?" And I thought maybe I would . . . other people have given up their children, so it isn't something that might not
have happened.

That night she told a representative of the group that she wanted to
stay but that she wanted three things: to have dinner with her son each
night; to go to bed at midnight and get up at 7:00 AM instead of 3:00
AM or 4:00 AM (members of the group had been averaging from four
to six hours of sleep for over a year); and to have some time for herself
to swim and garden. She was challenged, "Clara, if you had to let go
of those things for the group, would you do it?" Clara replied angrily,
"I don't know why I should! I don't know why it has to be that way!"
The response was, "Well, you'd better think about it some more."

That was the night, really. As soon as I hung up the phone I went
upstairs and called a close friend who was outside the group. It happened very fast. She was someone who had been in a spiritual group.
She had known Alex and something about Life Force, so I knew she'd

be someone who would understand the spiritual commitment we had made; I didn't want to talk to someone who would be critical of all that . . .

   She was wonderful. She didn't just say, "leave," or anything. It was like a little crack opened. I said, "Just talk, just keep talking." So she said, "I've made this commitment to my family and I'm committed to our work as a spiritual group, as well." It was like the sky opened a little bit and I said, "Just keep saying more things," and she did. She said things that somehow made me know that I wasn't going to need to give up my spiritual commitment if I left . . . that there were many ways to free your soul . . . one could live a family life and that her caring for her children was part of her commitment to God and her commitment to her husband was part of that, too . . . and I would say, "I hope I'll be able to help people," and she said, "Clara, you already are . . . you already have helped many people," . . . things like that. . . . It was very, very important. And I hung up the phone and then I called her back ten minutes later and said, "Say some more things," and the crack got a little bigger.

Clara stayed up all night. Over and over, she played a tape of Mother Theresa talking about working with the poor, about kindness and Christ.

   It was sort of lovely to be close to that . . . to get some perspective. I could feel my response . . . wanting to heal and wanting to help. She was expressing my resonance with that, particularly the kindness . . . the kindness was all gone from the group by that time . . . just the gentle kindness I could feel, that I have and that somehow I had betrayed a lot during that time. So I listened to that tape . . . and then at one point I realized that the energy that I thought we were working with was in me, and that it would be in me even if I left the group. . . . I really had that experience, it was not just mental but all the way through me. When I realized that, I knew I could leave. I decided that was what I needed to do. I wrote a note: "I'm leaving the group. It is no longer a place that I want to be. I don't know what my service will be but I know that it needs to involve family and children more than this does." The next morning I dropped it in Alex's box and then I ran into Hugh almost immediately afterward.

Leaving was not joyful. Clara had joined Life Force because it made her feel loved and accepted, and it had been a way to help others. At this point she felt worthless, evil, and alone, and she doubted her ability to help anyone.

For a week I didn't tell anyone that I had left except Hugh. I just sat upstairs in a chair. . . . The first night I kept feeling that there was an enormous cloud of darkness just off my fingertips or on the edge of the room or certainly down in the direction of the Center. I had to keep it out, I had to protect myself from it. . . . I made a circle on the floor of a book of Gandhi and the Mother Theresa tape and I had a picture by Kathe Kollwitz of Mary and Elizabeth embracing . . . like a protective circle, good friends who had made a spiritual commitment to the world. I wanted them near me. The great fear was that I was bad. The picture of my future was that I would do penance . . . redeem myself in some way. I volunteered at a nearby hospital on the cancer ward and I worked there three mornings a week for the next few months. I just wanted to give people water and hold their hand. . . . I was still grappling with maybe I was really bad. . . . I wrote and wrote and wrote about it in my journal. I kept wishing someone would tell me that I was good and I also knew that that wouldn't do it. Eventually [in meditation] I was saying to something deep in myself, "I really do want to help," and I heard a voice say, "I know you do." And then it was all right . . . that was the turning point . . . then I knew that I was still good, that I was still the person who wanted to love and wanted to make my commitment to love. I didn't really wonder about it after that time. Working it through on my own was real important . . . something I had to figure out for myself that I don't think anyone else could have told me. I feel proud of that moment . . . of staying with that.

Clara had hoped that when she left the group, Hugh would also. But he did not, although he knew that as long as he stayed he would not see his child, since contact was not allowed between those in the group and those who had left.

HUGH: For some reason, I'd made a vow to stay a year, no matter what happened. I was going to go on and do great spiritual work.

Hugh was expected to have no contact with Clara, to give her no money, no support, just to wipe the slate clean. He was told that Clara had left the group because she had become identified with her evil part, that all the good qualities she had were left in the group.

HUGH: Luckily we had this wonderful friend . . . I wasn't about to abandon Clara so I sent money through her. There was contact with this woman friend from both of us. I would go there for dinner and we would talk a little bit about Clara and I would say, "Is Clara angry at me?" And she said, "Oh, Hugh, Clara loves you so much!" She would say the same thing to Clara. . . . So, slowly, over those months there was an indirect healing or reconnection.

After several months Clara sent a letter to Hugh through their mutual friend, secretly, apologizing for what had happened and sharing her distress over the events. Hugh phoned Clara and over the next few weeks they had several clandestine contacts.

HUGH: There was the beginning of trust and love flowing again between us . . . and Clara asking me some wonderful questions. . . . Not pushing me but saying, "What do you see? Is this the kind of group that Christ would be near? Is this really the way people who love each other treat one another?"

Hugh also contacted others who had left the group, setting up clandestine meetings at street corners or in cars.

Having gained in confidence from these contacts, Hugh then wrote to the executive committee stating that he needed to make an arrangement to take care of his son, to spend time with him, and that he also needed time for his music. Hugh was immediately put back into quarantine.

HUGH: It was the sixth or seventh time it happened—this was the first time I wasn't paralyzed with fear. I started cataloging my fears . . . I would sit there in quarantine in my room and write down all the different levels of fear I had. It was fascinating . . . fear of inadequacy, fear of damnation, fear of becoming just a vegetable. They were still giving me tapes of the meetings and I would listen to the tapes and I'd draw a line down the middle of the page and I'd write down on one side the world view that was being put out in the group that I could buy, and then I would write down on the other side what I could see actually happening. . . . It was fascinating because the things that Alex was describing, what these subjective [evil] entities were supposedly doing "out there" to us were precisely the things that he was doing in relationship to the group, right there. You could hear it on the tapes. I was holding these two worldviews side by side. That was where I felt the most schizophrenic, the most stressed. . . . I had this image of the back of an envelope with "I quit" on it, and I knew that if I began to crack that I would grab the nearest piece of paper, write "I quit" on it, stick it in Alex's mailbox and run out the door. But I wanted to find out as much as I could about what was going on before I left.

During the last year of Hugh's involvement, the group and Alex Monroe had deteriorated markedly. Paranoia pervaded the members' lives. Fantasies had acquired so much power that even sensate perception changed to accommodate the group's delusional world. Alex's focus on past lives had become more pervasive. His fantasies included a particularly malignant creature who was cruel, cunning, scheming, manipulative, and very smart, very beautiful, and an assortment of other characters, including devils with wings—a complete cosmos.

HUGH: People would begin to see them [the devils], and then call teams to protect them. We had all become very paranoid by then . . . I would spend hours . . . fourteen or fifteen hours in a row on the phone, protecting [group members] and fighting some subjective entity who was attacking somebody else. Barbara Monroe was one who seemed to be attacked a lot . . . she would call and say this particular entity, "Charlie," a big, black devil with wings, was attacking her . . . we would call in the forces of light and we would do a visualization. To fight the dark force you would bring in an angel of light, an archangel with a sword . . . light against dark in imagery. Barbara would get better, or she would get over her migraine headache or whatever. . . . Each person had their kind of private devils. It would happen among the executive committee and then we'd hear about it and have to clean it up. Each of the executive committee had his or her own [devil]. One had a panther-like cat, another this disembodied head, and another this dark archangel, and so forth.

Such so-called subjective work had come to occupy more and more of the group's time, particularly as a team of three or four members would be giving support to meetings or processing sessions by conducting a group visualization of their own. Subjective work was extended to cover phone calls, not only within the group, but to people outside the group as well. The members could not go to sleep until protective measures were taken for members of the inner circle and for anyone designated as having trouble.

CLARA: At the end of a day's work, there would be a team that would call you and say, "Before you go to bed tonight, would you 'clean up' Erica? Would you 'clean up' Debbie? 'Clean up' their clothes and shop and stuff?" There would be this protection we would put around the whole group before we could go to sleep and that would take forever . . . we'd be falling asleep.

HUGH: By the end of my time [in the group] we were doing it [subjective work] almost exclusively, fourteen, fifteen, sixteen hours a day. The executive committee was so paranoid and Alex was so paranoid he stayed in his room the whole time and everyone else was in apartments and the executive committee couldn't even meet in the same room together for fear that they would do numbers on each other, trips, power trips, seduction trips, so forth. . . . There were always teams "cleaning up" the executive committee so the executive committee could meet. Alex, also, was having to work with all four of them, there were only four executives left by then [all women] . . . the men were gone . . . Alex and his women were all that was left.

HUGH: I knew I was going to leave . . . the more I talked to Clara, the clearer that became. I waited ten days and then a phone call came in the afternoon . . . it was Alex and another executive, supposedly to talk about my letter. So they started in . . . I was able to stand up to Alex for about an hour. I told him, "I'm in touch with my soul but I see the group over here in a corner, I'm no longer connected to the group." He was furious . . . he attacked . . . I stood up to it for a while and then I just went [under] . . . as we all did. . . . The best you could do was pretend . . . just try and bear it and hope it would be over soon.

The processing proceeded—all by telephone. Alex portrayed Clara and Hugh's son, David, as interpenetrated by a devil. It was done through suggestions:

ALEX: Are you thinking of going back to Clara?

HUGH: Well, that would depend but I certainly want to have some contact with her around David.

ALEX: Close your eyes and see Clara.

Alex would then evoke from Hugh's memory all the negative things that Clara had done to him.

ALEX: How do you feel about that, Hugh?

HUGH: I feel angry.

Then Hugh was sent to the special catharsis room at the Center where he ventilated his anger at Clara for two hours.

HUGH: I knew there were two things going on. I was play acting it to some degree because I knew this was the kind of thing I would go through and on the other hand, it was so powerful, it was real. And it did reinforce once again, the negative image of Clara. It was a kind of shared fantasy of paranoia in which Alex's view of how things were would be infiltrated into the person's head through strong emotional reinforcement because he could get this anger out. . . . That night I got out a lot of rage at Clara which I am sure was connected with the fact that I felt she had betrayed me. Then he would feed the feeling of betrayal and anger with images and slanted questions, "Who do you see behind Clara?" knowing full well and my knowing full well that it was supposed to be one of Alex's imaginary characters. "And what's she doing?" And then, "What do they [Clara and David] want to do to your heart? They don't want to love it do they?" It was that kind of leading question. He'd never say, "They want to eat your heart, Hugh," he'd get you to say it and then he'd reinforce it. "Yes, yes, they want to eat your heart and it's wrong, Hugh; it's a sin. It's wrong to love them." Alex implied that Clara and David just wanted my money and were loving me in order to get my money and not for myself. "They don't deserve your love. They can't use your love. The people who need your love are the students in the training program." It was that kind of thing.

Alex would give [you] a choice, he would say, "Well, you don't want to live your life that way [selfishly], do you?" And you'd say, "No, no, I know I don't." "Well then, . . ." It was a kind of nod to psychological processing in terms of catharsis, making choices, intention, higher values, but it became increasingly Alex projecting whatever was in his mind into people.

The processing continued for eight hours. Although Hugh tried to fake compliance he was terrified of the strong images that had been summoned. He could not prevent Alex from affecting him.

I don't understand this, but this happened for other people, too, at the end of these eight hours there was this experience of love for Alex, and his love for me, and a kind of intimacy that was very compelling. I apologized to him for making it hard for him, that he'd had to spend these eight hours with me . . . and then he wept on the phone and I wept, and he said, "Oh, that helps so much," and I said how much I loved him.

I woke up the next morning and it was like I couldn't find my head. Everything that I had put together had been shattered. I had been really beat up . . . I had been under severe attack from people who thought they were saving me from the devil. Looking back it feels like a snake whispering in my ears for eight hours. This ear is still slightly deaf . . . the hearing has never totally come back on this side.

However, Hugh was prepared. He went back to the notes he had taken so carefully and reconstructed what had happened. The battle to leave was a struggle against intense fear.

The point of highest tension for me was to figure out what reality system did I want to commit to. Alex was saying, "You need to turn away from your child and Clara and never even think about them anymore. There should be no contact. Nothing. Just turn away." I was so afraid . . . fear of damnation is what it finally became and Alex would reinforce it . . . images of outer darkness, gnashing of teeth, just total and utter damnation . . . I had to go against that, I had to pit against that the principle that a father does not leave his child. I couldn't believe that God wanted me to leave my child for anything. I said, "Even if I'm damned forever, even if I'm going to be cast into outer darkness, I'm not going to turn against David." That saved me, woke me up. I'm so glad, I'm so grateful.

Despite this resolve, there were times during that last week when the pull of Alex and the group would threaten to overwhelm him. At one point Hugh phoned Clara in a panic.

I could feel a maelstrom, a vortex and I was going to lose my will and be sucked into the center of this thing . . . I could see in the center . . . this nice, cozy place, where all your needs were taken care of and it was loving. I remember writing down in big letters, "I've got to get out of here!"

In the last few weeks before leaving Life Force, Hugh was helped by talking with another group member, Jerry (although communication between them had been forbidden), about his perceptions of what Alex was doing.

At last there was contact with someone inside the group who saw things the way I did. There was just an explosion of talk . . . clandestine . . . after the work was over we'd call each other up and talk.

Finally, a week after the processing session, Hugh wrote a letter of resignation. The next morning, very early, he placed a copy on each member's doorstep and then left the city.

The word went out that I was the anti-Christ and that my resignation letter was to be picked up with tongs, put in another envelope, sealed, and burned. Everything I'd ever given to anybody—loaned a bed or a book or whatever—were to be destroyed or turned in. The interesting thing was that the people who were there were feeling closer and closer to the Christ while all this was going on.

Hugh stayed in communication with Jerry, helping him to leave also.

HUGH: [Jerry would say,] "I'm sitting here and my whole body is shaking and trembling with fear . . . it's rising off the bed . . . my heart is shaking. . . . if I bought the system, I would say that you were the devil and you were seducing me away from the group."

And I would say, "Okay, what's true?" I'd just sit there. "What's true?" And then he would gradually [say,] "I know that's not true. . . ." We spent a long time on the phone where he would go through the same process that I'd gone through. It was just like a buffer zone of terror around the group that a person had to cross. It was almost necessary to have a person on the outside.

Jerry left the organization soon after. Hugh's leaving set off a chain of resignations; each person who departed helped others to leave. A packet of letters of resignation was circulated among the graduate students, most of whom then left. With so many of the staff gone, the graduate school closed. Shortly thereafter, Alex and the remaining group members went underground, moving to another city where they were said to be spending their entire time processing each other.

The story of Hugh and Clara Robinson illustrates what can happen when thought and perception come to be controlled by desire and fear. The psychological damage the Robinsons suffered in the cult process was extensive; their sense of self-worth, emotional stability, and relationships with those closest to them were badly battered. Indeed, many months after leaving the group, the Robinsons were still recovering from the trauma of the experience.

Readers may wonder how different Hugh and Clara were from themselves. After all, prior to joining Life Force, Clara had become very anxious; Hugh was discontented, uncomfortable with his life. Yet to us in the seminar, the Robinsons did not seem very different from most people. After additional interviews (which I conducted myself), I found no reason to change that assessment.

Although the world of Life Force may seem alien to most of us, in a number of important ways Hugh and Clara's experience was not qualitatively different from that which occurs in everyday society, although it was more radical, more intense, less subject to moderating influences, and, consequently, more pathological.

Analysis of Hugh and Clara's experience and that of others involved with cults reveals four basic behaviors found in extreme form in cults: compliance with the group, dependence on a leader, devaluing the outsider, and avoiding dissent. These behaviors are not distinct and independent but interrelated. In my view, they arise in part from what I refer to as the dependency dream, the regressive wish for security that uses the family as a model, creating an authoritarian leadership structure (the parent) and a close-knit, exclusive group (the children). Since the leader-parent has many of the insecurities of the follower-child, reality must be distorted by both to maintain the child's illusion (or wish) that the parent can always provide protection, that he or she has no weaknesses. Dissent is stifled because it casts doubt on the perfection of the leader and the special status of the group. Group compliance preserves security by supporting the beliefs crucial to the fantasy of superiority, beliefs that also explain the powers and entitlement of the leader and can no more be challenged than he or she. Outsiders, non-believers, are excluded and devalued for they do not believe what the group believes; if the group and leader are superior, the outsider is inferior.

Because group boundaries are more permeable in everyday society, hidden ("normal") cult behavior is not as intense as in overt cults, and the relative importance of one or the other of these interlocking behaviors may vary considerably depending on the social organization being studied.

In the next chapters, I will describe how cult behaviors are manifested in everyday life in our society, using examples from large corporations, religion, psychiatry, the media, and government. I do not mean to imply that other levels of motivation are not active also, but they are conscious. The danger of the longing for the back seat of the car is that because it is usually unconscious, it can powerfully influence us in ways that are not recognized.

We recognize an overt threat from powerful authorities, be it loss of job, injury to self or loved ones, or imprisonment. Likewise, most people are acutely aware of the lure of money, fame, and power. However, we are not accustomed to recognizing the effect on us of the threats and rewards of childhood's world: the parental frown or the parental smile, the invitation to play or the exclusion from a game, the blissful comfort of being cared for.

The dependency dream acts as an unseen regressive force, shaping our behavior to accomplish the desires of childhood while we are pursuing the goals of adults. It produces unconscious submission to the beliefs and demands of authorities. It leads us to seek reassurance by repeating dogma, to attack outsiders, to ignore and devalue dissenting opinions. Unwillingness to disrupt the fantasy that we have a wise, strong parent in charge leads us to accept the limits of debate established by authorities and the beliefs upon which those authorities depend. Thus, the anxiety evoked by a cult situation is not often recognized for what it is. Even when fear of the leader is conscious, a person is not usually aware that it may be based on the persistence in adulthood of a child's desire and vulnerability, as much as on any realistic need or possibility of reprisal.

Although a deprived or traumatic childhood may result in greater vulnerability to cult manipulation or deceit, the experience of childhood itself renders us susceptible to the blissful promise of a safe, secure way to return home. A continuum of behavior exists, from the Peoples Temple to Life Force, to rigid religious groups, corporate cultures, professional societies, and ordinary us/them categories.

What I wish to stress is not that every group is a cult, but that cult thinking is the effect of psychological forces endemic to the human mind, and that these forces operate in the everyday life of each of us; they distort perception, bias thinking, and inculcate belief. Our own behavior brings us closer to the experience of Hugh and Clara than we would like to believe.

3 Compliance with the Group

HUMAN BEINGS ARE SOCIAL BEINGS. Mother, father, siblings, grand-parents, and other relatives form our first social group. The family into which we are born has enormous influence upon us, not only because a long and complex learning process takes place before we attain adult-hood and self-sufficiency, but also because the family becomes the par-adigm for other social groups. In fact, most social groups share char-acteristics of family groups with members who occupy dominant (parent) and subordinate (child) roles. By considering the character-istics that social groups share with families, we can understand why individuals who are considered independent and adult outside the group may become dependent and childlike within it.

Of course, the family's adults—who transmit social attitudes, fears, and hopes to the child—are themselves subject to the influence of larger social units toward which they may have many of the same depend-ency feelings that their child has toward them. These overlapping ref-erence groups are composed of friends, colleagues, and/or people of similar religious and political persuasions. Reference groups influence our behavior greatly, although we may not be conscious of how and when this occurs.

Conformity to characteristic views, dress, and conduct differenti-ate social groupings, marking the most outwardly rebellious as well as the most conventional.[1] An amusing example comes from my own field of psychiatry. Janet Malcolm relates the experience of an analyst of the New York Psychoanalytic Institute who, shortly after he graduated, purchased a black-and-white herringbone tweed jacket which enormously pleased him. Two years later he met a fellow analyst wearing an almost identical jacket. "My colleague laughed and said, 'But, you know, everyone at the New York Psychoanalytic wears this kind of jacket.' So then I understood why I had felt so great about my jacket. I began to look around the Institute and, sure enough, the jacket was all over the place."[2]

Imitation of our peers is basic to learning and development and the reference group is an important influence throughout life. Social psychologist Albert Bandura and his colleagues were able to cure children of nursery school age of fear of dogs by the simple procedure of having them watch another child playing happily with a dog. Even when films were used instead of actual demonstrations, the procedure worked. Even more striking was the research of psychologist Robert O'Connor on socially withdrawn school children who typically stayed on the fringes of peer group activities. Believing that their behavior predicted a pattern of lifelong isolation and social unease, and trying to change that pattern, O'Connor put together a film composed of eleven different nursery school scenes. Each scene showed a different solitary child observing a social activity and then joining in, to everyone's pleasure. O'Connor tried the film on a group of the most severely withdrawn children from four nursery schools. The results were impressive.

After watching the film, the isolates immediately began to interact with their peers at a level equal to that of the "normal" children in the schools. Even more astonishing was what O'Connor found when he returned to the schools six weeks later to observe. While the withdrawn children who had not seen O'Connor's film remained as isolated as ever, those who had viewed it were now leading their schools in amount of social activity. It seems that this twenty-three-minute movie, viewed just once, was enough to reverse a potential pattern of lifelong maladaptive behavior.[3]

Yet, as we know, the power of group influence has its negative side and not only in cults. For example, research indicates that the reason a group of bystanders may not come to the aid of a victim is not that they are indifferent, heartless, or "numbed by urban living," but because in uncertain situations each person looks to others for cues as to how to interpret and react to what is happening. Each person's passivity reinforces that of others. In contrast, when researchers enacted an "emergency" in the presence of a single bystander, that person invariably responded helpfully, whether in a city or not. Clearly, reliance on social cues, not empathy, is the issue.

Robert Cialdini, an experimental social psychologist, explains the group's influence on our behavior as being utilitarian:

> The tendency to see an action as more appropriate when others are doing it works quite well normally. As a rule, we will make fewer mistakes by acting in accord with social evidence than contrary to it. Usually, when a lot of people are doing something, it is the right thing to do.[4]

But every society provides numerous examples of group influence that turned out to be injurious to the group itself, as well as unfair and harmful to others. How and why do groups affect their members so strongly?

THE POWER OF GROUPS

The remarkable influence of groups upon their members has been of interest to psychologists and psychiatrists for a long time. Gustave Le Bon was one of the first to study the behavior of people in crowds and mobs. Writing in 1895 about such situations, he described "the disappearance of the conscious personality, the predominance of the unconscious personality, the turning by means of suggestion and contagion of feelings and ideas in an identical direction, the tendency to immediately transform the suggested ideas into acts."[5]

Sigmund Freud believed that these characteristics could be explained as a regression to a primitive mental activity, that of the primal horde. "The primitive form of human society was that of a horde ruled over despotically by a powerful male . . . Just as primitive man survives potentially in every individual, so the primal horde may arise once more out of any random collection."[6]

Freud went on to emphasize:

> . . . the contrivance by means of which an artificial group is held together and the constitution of the primal horde. We have seen that with an army and a Church this contrivance is the illusion that the leader loves all of the individuals equally and justly. But this is simply an idealistic remodeling of the state of affairs in the primal horde, where all of the sons knew that they were equally persecuted by the primal father, and feared him equally.[7]

Freud's analysis—its exclusively male focus aside—would seem to have applicability in the case of the Life Force group, where the initial feeling of the members of being loved by Alex gave way to fear of him.

Since Freud, the theory of group psychology has been expanded. British psychoanalyst Wilfred Bion, drawing on Melanie Klein's ideas about primitive psychological defenses in the infant and young child, studied small-group phenomena and concluded that groups tend to adopt, unconsciously, one of three primitive emotional states—dependency, pairing, or fight-flight. Bion called these states basic assumptions, and thought of them as expressive of disowned impulses. He saw any group as likely to exhibit irrational behavior, indicating that one of the three assumptions is operating. What Bion designates as the dependency-assumption group is a very good description of the state of mind prevailing in cults:

> The essential aim [of the dependency-assumption group] . . . is to attain security through and have its members protected by one individual. It assumes that this is why the group has met. The members act as if they know nothing, as if they are inadequate and immature creatures. Their behavior implies that the leader, by contrast, is omnipotent and omniscient.[8]

Object relations theorist D. W. Winnicott has suggested that the group may represent a transitional object for its members who express regressive themes appropriate to that stage of development. Going further, Jungian analyst Arthur Colman, drawing on the work of Margaret Mahler, has proposed that group consciousness is a developmental phase prior to full individuation.[9]

All these theorists endeavor to explain the powerful effect of groups from the point of view of the psychology of the individuals that compose them. However, from a sociobiological point of view, there is another basis for understanding why the group should be so influential: human survival has been enhanced by the tendency for families to combine in bands or tribes for mutual protection and support. As banishment from the larger group could endanger an individual's survival, an acute sensitivity to the group's wishes and requirements probably carried an evolutionary advantage. Socially aware, adept individuals would eventually dominate the genetic pool through the process of natural selection. Perhaps in this way the human race has developed a high awareness of the wishes, fears, and requirements of the groups on which each person depends. Such an evolutionary process may explain why certain basic group reactions and fantasies (such as those described by Bion) seem to take place regardless of the member's actual family experience.

Certainly, whatever theoretical model or models one might prefer, the desire for group approval and the fear of disapproval remain with us as very powerful controlling forces. In the Robinsons' case, Hugh's testimony makes clear how much his need for the group's approval influenced him, especially when he was in quarantine, and Clara recalled how seductive it was for the group to praise her while criticizing Hugh. Furthermore, numerous experiments show how a group can change the perceptions of its members, can even foster and maintain a bizarre, paranoid worldview such as that which developed within the Life Force executive group.

We can feel secure in the protection provided by a group but that protection has its price. Compliance with the group often extends further than acceptance of the group's views to include participation in the attack on deviants by subtle (or not so subtle) disapproval, punishment, or rejection of any member who voices criticism of the consensus or disagrees with the leader. The dissident is criticized as disloyal, lacking commitment, interfering with the important work of the group.

As a psychotherapist, I frequently work with people oppressed by a punitive, controlling internal figure who lashes them with guilt and mocks with disapproval. Exploring the reason for this oppression, we often find that its purpose is to ensure conformity to the group upon whose approval they depend and whose rejection they fear.

Although most social groups encourage dependency and compliance in civilized ways, the basic pattern can usually be discerned.

THE THREAT OF CONFLICTING LOYALTIES

Pressures encouraging dependency, present in most groups, are intensified in a cult. As we saw in the case of Hugh and Clara, extreme dependence on the cult is fostered by isolating the member from other sources of self-esteem, financial support, and emotional closeness. Consequently, the cult's ability to reward or punish is markedly enhanced. With this in mind it is not surprising that a particularly pernicious feature of cults—and often an index of their power over their members— is the attack on couples and families. In the case of Life Force, not a single couple who began with the group survived intact, even the marriage of Alex and Barbara Monroe failed. This destructive effect is characteristic of the stronger cults; the power of the leader and the sense of security of the group are diminished by any strong social bonds that set up conflicting loyalties. (Hugh and Clara's enduring bonds to their child and to each other eventually provided the motivation to break from the group.) Thus, powerful cult groups often attack the couple through arranged marriages, the breaking of love relationships by order of the leader or the group, pressure toward group marriage or chastity, sexual relationships with the leader, and/or interference with the bonds between parents and children. In her study of communes and utopian communities, sociologist Rosabeth Kanter described how in the previous century such groups coped with the threat to cohesiveness posed by two-person intimacy:

> Successful nineteenth century groups often discouraged couples in one of two extreme and experientially opposite ways—either through free love, including group marriage, in which every member was expected to have intimate sexual relations with all others, or through celibacy, in which no member could have sexual relations with any other.[10]

She cites the Oneida community, which had been notorious for its practice of free love:

> Every member had sexual access to every other with his or her consent, while fidelity was negatively sanctioned; preference of one member for another was quickly discouraged. When two members of the community showed a marked preference of one member for one another, they were asked to mate with two others.[11]

In such communities, ties between parents and children were minimized by varying degrees of communal childcare and by restricted contact between mother and child. In the Life Force group this was accomplished by making inordinate demands on Clara's time and devaluing her contribution as a mother, even labeling it selfish.

The weakening of family structures is not only an issue of loyalty. The role of parent and the roles of husband and wife are adult roles, whereas in a cult the leader and the group together constitute a parent-child structure in which adult autonomy has no place. For this reason it is in the cult's interest to foster the regression of its members to a pre-adult phase of psychosexual development, and such a regression is usually easy to observe. A family unit resists this push.

The attack on couples and families is usually restricted to tightly controlled groups that set themselves off from the surrounding society. Seldom is it a significant factor in ordinary society. However, the weakening of ties to others so as to strengthen dependency on the group and leader can be observed in strongly authoritarian political systems, such as that which prevailed in Germany's Third Reich. The Hitler Youth were encouraged to regard parents as potential enemies of the glorious new Germany, to inform on them and to turn them in to the Gestapo for comments critical of the Nazi regime. Many did so. Parents came to fear and distrust their children, while the children scorned their parents as being weak, obstructionist, or traitors.[12] Mao Tse-tung encouraged a similar split between the generations of China.

THE CONVERSION EXPERIENCE

Compliance and dependency can be strongly enhanced by the group's eliciting a powerful emotional experience. Lowell Streiker, a researcher who interviewed converts to revivalism, gives a composite description of a conversion experience as it typically occurs in a small revivalist group or church:

> The prospect is directly confronted with his sins. His physical and psychic space are invaded by these self-confident strangers. He is discomforted and thrown off balance. He becomes anxious. The group tells him that his feelings are caused by his sinfulness. He is overcome with guilt and sadness. He realizes that his life is not working. Eagerly he confesses his shortcomings—sexual lapses, lies, petty thievery, drug abuse, and so forth. Guided by the group, he prays that God will forgive him and receive him as His child. He is urged, "Ask Jesus to come into your heart." He does, and the inner turmoil subsides. The recruit senses an inner release and relief. The hugs and congratulations of the group tell him that he belongs, that he has identity, that he is accepted. Many ecstatic converts report, "It was as though a great weight had been lifted from my shoulders."[13]

Streiker suggests that such groups create an unbearable tension in the person on whom they are focusing, and that the sudden release from that tension—"accepting the Lord into your heart" or "surrender to Jesus"—is interpreted as a spiritual experience, being "born again." He goes on to comment, "When Jesus told Nicodemus of the need to be "born again" he did not badger his hearer until he underwent a group-coerced, programmed, stereotyped purgation."[14]

Of course, to be born again does not require a specifically Christian context. Listen again to Clara Robinson:

> So I went up towards the sun and there was this wise man and he said to me, "My child", and I climbed in his lap, like a child—he was very much like a father—as I retell it I realize that . . . I just felt like I was home. . . . I felt a downflow of love and affection that I have never felt before or since. . . . It was that experience that made me feel that I needed to do more of whatever this system was.

Groups may enhance compliance and dependency by producing a variety of altered states of consciousness that are easily misinterpreted to conform with the beliefs and interests of the group. Hugh and Clara Robinson always had an intuitive sense of a larger reality that was very important to them. That perception was confused with unresolved dependency longings, leading them to interpret the initial guided daydream as being spiritual and to accept the Monroes as guides or agents in that domain. A variety of techniques—chanting, singing, dancing, sleep deprivation, meditation—can produce a state of consciousness quite impressive to the participant. The event may then be offered as proof of the group's value or the leader's spiritual power—the convert's wish to believe does the rest.

Demonstrations of psychic ability are especially potent in this respect, and Yogic disciplines, in particular, seem to have a technology for producing phenomena unexplainable by current scientific knowledge. Some years ago, while investigating a popular Eastern cult, I underwent an initiation in which a Yogi placed his hand on my head and I then experienced a spot of intense white light blazing briefly in the center of my mind—or so it seemed. This was interpreted (by the cult) as contact with the divine and proof that the guru was a new messiah. I still don't understand how the man did it, but the spot of light was just that—a spot of light—and no more a demonstration of the divine than turning on the faucet would be to someone who knows nothing about plumbing. Indeed, the mystical literature warns repeatedly that such experiences are distractions and should be ignored.[15] (Nevertheless, this particular group's converts eagerly practiced the prescribed meditations hoping to repeat the experience and rushed to take part in any further initiations that were made available to them.)

Unfortunately, legitimate but subtle intimations of the spiritual that may have led a convert to search for a group and teacher may be displaced by such dramatic alterations of consciousness, which can then become a further basis for control. Just as the group's emotional support and validation can be provided or withdrawn, so can the dramatic pseudo-spiritual experiences. Before long, the positive force of idealism and service that may have been foremost in a convert's mind when joining a cult becomes corrupted by fear of deprivation and abandonment. As we saw in Life Force, idealistic concepts are then subverted when they are used to rationalize behavior a convert would have condemned before joining the group.

OPPRESSION BY CENSURE

A major way a group exerts power is through threat of censure and expulsion, classifying the deviant as bad. I had occasion to learn about this firsthand when I became involved in the anti-nuclear movement. (At that time I would not have believed that liberals such as myself could behave like cult members, although I was certain that right-wingers did.) The story is worth telling because it may connect with the reader's own prejudices and provide an experience of the very dynamic I am discussing.

In the 1980s, when Russia was the focus of our fears, the threat of a nuclear war—accidental or otherwise—was very real, and some felt such a horror was imminent. I responded by becoming active in spreading the word about the enormous danger and the immediate steps that should be taken. (This was not a new role for me; I had been active in the 1960s in the effort to stop the atmospheric testing of nuclear weapons. Now the menace was worse and the catastrophic aspects more overwhelming.) I raised questions with other activists about what action people might take to increase their chances of survival if a nuclear war did occur. I was told that there was nothing that could be done; shelters were described as useless and prevention of nuclear war as the only answer. Some speakers from Physicians for Social Responsibility declared that anyone who undertook civil defense planning was immoral, and engaged in "a highly unethical act."

These summary judgments were not convincing to me, and I began reading outside the peace-movement literature, encountering other points of view and other facts. Eventually, I came to the judgment that regional food stockpiles would save millions of lives if a war did occur and that establishing such stockpiles would not accelerate the arms race or give people a false sense of security, but would be a logical and appropriate response to a very real danger. Furthermore, I believed that people should be told the less alarming facts about radiation danger and about what protection a shelter could and could not offer.

When I mentioned these ideas to my friends in the peace movement, they would draw back slightly, their eyes would narrow, and I could see them mentally remove my name from the file of "good guys" and transfer it to the one marked "bad guys." (Perhaps you, the reader, have been having a similar reaction.)

I promoted a lecture about protection against a variety of radiation hazards, including nuclear explosions. Almost no one came, except some protesters from the peace movement. With the radiologist who gave the lecture, I later appeared on a radio talk show. It was clear the host found it hard to grasp that although I was in favor of stockpiling food, a civil defense measure, I was opposed to the further development of nuclear weapons and favored a nuclear freeze. He had assumed, as did others, that I must be a hawk. A cult-like propensity for a black-and-white division of the world was all too obvious.

This publicity, along with an interview published in a local newspaper, generated a response whose character and vehemence caught me by surprise. I was roundly attacked. No one from the peace movement asked me why I thought what I did. They weren't curious at all; they had simply decided I had become a hardliner, an immoral survivalist. The arguments that advanced against my views seemed simplistic and illogical, much like the recitations of dogma I was familiar with from my study of religious cults.

In addition to seeing cult processes at work in others, I became aware that I was influenced by them. I began to avoid mentioning my views to acquaintances and even some friends, for fear of being cast out. Educational as the experience proved, being regarded as a bad guy within my own group was quite unpleasant. At one public hearing where I testified, I was attacked by a peace movement contingent that used the same rhetoric that I had used in the past as part of that same group. It was startling to be on the receiving end, to be the object of the glaring hostile eyes and the impassioned appeals to humanity. Ruefully, I realized that in the past I had been similarly self-indulgent in obtaining the emotional satisfaction that springs from being righteous in a good cause. I would not have known that I was to some degree a member of a cult had I not challenged my group's dogma.

DEGREES OF DEPENDENCE

Compliance with a group increases with one's psychological and economic dependence on it. This can be seen in many social institutions, including the corporations that dominate modern economic life.

Sociologist Diane Margolis studied the managers at a large corporation and found that the one effect of frequent transfers was to decrease a husband and wife's involvement in local politics and community life and to increase their dependence on the friends and activities of their particular corporate world. Moreover, they learned to buy their homes with a view to resell and this tended to place them in housing areas occupied by other corporation managers. Economic and social segregation played an important role in the corporation's becoming, for many managers, the chief source of self-esteem, companionship, and personal expression. For the managers of many corporations:

> . . . needs usually fulfilled by human relationships become increasingly difficult to satisfy because almost all relationships outside their nuclear families are distant and fleeting. So like half-starved people

who in the absence of proteins will fatten but not nourish themselves on starches, managers and their families hunger for goods money cannot buy, but reach for those it can. Each year salary increases put these within easier reach, and the manager's family finds that every purchase just whets the appetite for the next. . . . He knew he was in a game he could never win, but he played on. For him it was the only game in town.[16]

To leave the company would mean all that sacrifice has been in vain; security must be given up. Wishful thinking tends to replace critical assessment just as it did with the Robinsons who also had to face giving up a "warm cocoon." With few connections to the outside world that world can easily appear less desirable—and the corporation more valuable—than it is.

CAREER REALITIES AND CULT DEMANDS

Although corporations do not attack the family directly in the manner of cults such as Life Force, most of them do require the subordination of the manager's family's needs to those of the corporation. This sacrifice is demanded as the price for career advancement.

A common practice is to promote managers by transferring them every year or two to positions in other parts of the country. Then their positions are filled by others who are moved in; a game of musical chairs takes place.

Certainly, it is in the corporation's interest to give managers wide experience and also to test their commitment to the company; however, the interests of the managers' children are served poorly. (Although corporations have begun paying more attention to this problem, the transfer is still a standard feature of corporate life.) Indeed, in my psychotherapy practice I often encounter people who have been socially impaired by frequent family moves that made them perpetually new kids on the block; just when friendships were established, their families would move again. Such children learn to limit their friendships to avoid the pain of loss and tend to interpret other children's reserve toward them when they arrive in a new town as indicating that they are not likable. For many wives the process is almost as painful:

> If people know you're going to move, they start to disengage them-
> selves from you, too . . . you find them backing off. . . . You start
> finding out that they're not there anymore. They're busy. And they're
> busy with things they know they're going to be doing after you've
> left. You notice it . . . people starting to draw back. And the kids, I
> know, would say they couldn't get any friends to come and play. The
> other kids would suddenly be busy with somebody else, even though
> they've always been with them. Their friends were starting to find
> somebody else because after all, "she's leaving." [17]

Frequent transfers are also ruinous to a spouse's career ambitions. The wife of a Schlumberger manager stationed in Cairo summed it up:

> Sometimes you really feel lost. . . . The man has a job to do. You
> have nothing to do. So you have babies to keep you busy. Or you
> join a club. If you say, "I want to have a career of my own," and say
> you don't want to go where your husband goes, then you're headed
> for the divorce courts. [8]

Commitment to the corporation is also measured by a manager's willingness to take work home at night and on weekends and to be absent from his family on frequent business trips. In the competition for a manager's time, energy, and attention the corporation is out to win. Conflicts that arise between family needs and corporate needs—which may have the look of accidental occurrences—are sometimes deliberate tests of the person's commitment, the outcomes of which are carefully noted. The manager who chooses family over the corporation fails the test, as does the family.

Furthermore, wives may become unpaid company employees as they fall in line to support the careers of their husbands:

> They [the managers] are . . . corporate men, not family men. Wives
> must actively subordinate themselves to the husbands' work aims or,
> at the very least, not interfere with them. The key to an effective part-
> nership . . . (would be) the degree to which the wife actively adopted

the corporate goals and skillfully aided the husband in that direction. This makes the wife a kind of high-class assistant bound by marriage rather than salary but otherwise facilitating the work goals with the same sense of efficiency the husband would expect of his secretary and other office personnel. The all-embracing demands of corporate life do not permit distraction.[19]

Within the corporate culture of many companies, it is assumed that the corporate goals and the husband's career should have first priority in much the same way that Life Force and other cults regard their own activities as primary and the competing demands of marriage and family as distinctly secondary. As Harold Geneen, former chief executive officer of ITT put it: "The first requirement of a senior executive is instant availability. He must put his firm above his family; he must be prepared to go anywhere at any time, or simply to wait around in case he is needed."[20]

Just as the commitment and spiritual worth of the Robinsons were judged by the extent to which they sacrificed their marriage relationship and their child's needs to the purposes of their group, the loyalty of the corporate manager is usually measured by the acceptance of corporation priorities over anything else in life.

Of course, corporations vary in their demands, and some managers sacrifice their family's interests over and above what the corporation requires. Personal ambition can take a toll without any pressure at all from corporate authority.

CORPORATE CULTURE OR CORPORATE CULT?

Studies of corporations generally recognized as continuously innovative, with long-term records of growth and profitability, indicate that a strong corporate culture is a key ingredient in their success. By corporate culture we mean a set of values or principles that permeate a company and form the guidelines for decision-making at all levels.[21] The inculcation of those values constitutes a process of corporate socialization that seems to be responsible for the survival from generation to generation of many large business organizations, providing stability and dependable responses. "What emerges in firms as different as AT&T is from Procter & Gamble, as Morgan Guaranty is from IBM or Delta Airlines, is an awesome internal consistency which powerfully shapes behavior."[22]

For example, IBM teaches all employees its three "Basic Beliefs": 1) respect for the individual, 2) best possible service to our customers, 3) every task performed in a superior manner. Delta Airlines "Family Feeling" and AT&T's "Universal Service" are other examples of core values taught to all employees and taken seriously. Although the phrases sound like platitudes, within the corporation they are very meaningful.

These "significant meanings," "shared values," or "spiritual fabric" have been described as superordinate goals guiding the entire organization. They play a very practical role because employees must often make decisions on their own; as long as they are guided by the corporate shared values, decisions are likely to fit in with company policy.[23]

Achieving a strong corporate culture that managers really care about requires a process of indoctrination to convert a recruit to the corporation's point of view. Richard Pascale lists a number of steps in the process of "socialization," including "humility-inducing experiences:"

> Humility inducing experiences in the first months on the job precipitate self-questioning of prior behavior, beliefs and values. A lowering of individual self-comfort and self-complacency promotes openness toward accepting the organization's norms and values.
>
> Most strong culture companies get the new hire's attention by pouring on more work than can possibly get done. IBM and Morgan Guaranty socialize extensively through training where "you work every night until 2:00 a.m. on your own material and then help others." . . . Humility tends to flourish under certain conditions; especially long hours of intense work that bring you to your limits. When vulnerability is high, one also becomes close to one's colleagues— and cohesiveness is intensified in pressure cooker environments where little opportunity is given to reestablish social distance and regain one's bearings. . . . Near identical patterns of long hours, exhausting travel schedules and extensive immersion in case work are true at the major consulting firms and law practices.[24]

The use of overwork is also a feature of extreme cults, as in the case of Life Force. An ex-convert from the Unification Church described what it was like there:

> Sleep especially, was viewed as an indulgence since God never slept in His efforts to save mankind. Sleep, more than food, thus came to represent the most sought-after "privilege" of a future life in the Kingdom of Heaven. The staff averaged three hours a night; newer Family would average six. Recognized but unspoken was a state of constant exhaustion in all righteous children of God.[25]

Overwork is part of many initiations. Army recruits rise early and are put through long forced marches. Doctors during internship may get only one night's sleep every two days. Overwork facilitates submission through a kind of anesthesia produced by exhaustion; rebellion takes energy.[26] Immersion in the newly joined world to the exclusion of other influences is also important in initiations. Consider this description of how Schlumberger, until recently one of the most successful corporations of our time, initiates its engineers:

> Like military recruits who go through basic training together, they became a clan. They worked sometimes seven days a week for two straight months. They lived, ate, drank, showered, watched video cassettes, and vacationed together. They swapped stories about their work. For months at a time, the only people they had contact with worked for Schlumberger or for an oil company.[27]

The resemblance of such initiations to the procedures of religious cults is striking. That the resulting corporate attitude evokes from observers the phrase "religious fervor" is not surprising. Indeed, some executives are quite explicit about the parallel with religion:

> People need to believe in something larger than themselves. To be successful . . . a corporation must learn from the Japanese that "we have the responsibility that religion used to have." A good company must not be just a slave to profits; it must strive to perform a service and to beat its competitors. But more . . . it must measure itself against a higher standard, seeking perfection.[28]

Terrance Deal and Allen Kennedy, who studied the cultures of eighty corporations, also spoke of the corporate religion they had observed: "The Catholic church has something in common with IBM, Mary Kay, McDonald's, the Polaris project, the U.S. Forest Service, and countless numbers of other successful organizations—all of them capture some of the same religious tone."[29]

At the same time, as in the case of Life Force, high purposes may be subverted, with destructive results. Thomas Peters and Robert Waterman, authors of *In Search of Excellence,* warn that:

> . . .the more worrisome part of a strong culture is the ever-present possibility of abuse. One of the needs filled by the strong excellent company cultures is the need most of us have for security. We will surrender a great deal to institutions that give us a sense of meaning and, through it, a sense of security.[30]

Richard Pascale and Anthony Athos, who wrote *The Art of Japanese Management,* sound an even stronger cautionary note:

> Having made the case for the importance of superordinate goals in motivating employees and sustaining an organization over time, we must note that a skillful grasp of the use of all of our seven variables can be directed toward truly tragic outcomes. The staggering horror of the Third Reich and the mass suicides in Guyana come to mind. It is not hard to imagine an indoctrination of people into some kind of corporate Hitler Youth Corps.[31]

In the case of cults, moral principles are often violated to further the cult's success. The leader and the members justify immoral actions as being necessary for the greater good that the cult will achieve: To make an omelet one must break eggs. Implied in this attitude is an assumption that the leader's aims are sublimely important, as is the welfare of the special group instrumental in accomplishing these great goals. Also implied is a lowering of the importance of any individual's welfare and a lowering still further of the worth of the outsider. Part of the attraction of believing the leader's views and actions to be of paramount importance is that the follower's own sense of importance is heightened. One might sense such a dynamic behind the arrogance and self-righteousness displayed by Oliver North at the Iran-contra hearings in 1987. (In 1989, with Reagan out of office, North took a different role, that of victim and scapegoat.)

Making the welfare of the corporation more important than anything else, believing in its overriding importance, is the qualitative equivalent to a cult's belief in its divine mission. Charles Wilson, former CEO of General Motors, put it succinctly in his famous assertion, "What's good for General Motors is good for the United States."

An appreciation of the power of cult dynamics may help us understand immoral corporate actions by people who outside the corporation conduct themselves differently. For example, according to Paul Brodeur (a *New Yorker* writer), the board of directors of the Johns Mansville company deliberately withheld from their workers evidence that asbestos was dangerous to their health, asserting that there was no threat when they knew there was a very serious problem indeed.[32] Another writer, Morton Mintz, has described the actions of the A. H. Robbins Company in not withdrawing the Dalkon shield (a birth control device) from the marketplace after they had evidence of its serious side effects.[33] One reads of the failure of numerous nuclear power plants to correct safety problems. The list is long. I suggest that "the Corporation" evokes a fantasy of "the Big Parent" in the minds of the board of directors as well as in middle management. They identify with it and are reassured by it; the corporation is the protector and must be protected. Just as saving the world was used as a justification for the Life Force group's cruelty to its members or saving souls is used to justify unethical and illegal actions by religious zealots, so the economic well-being of the corporation may come to be considered important enough to justify actions that would otherwise be abhorred.

SELF-DECEPTION AND COMPLIANCE

Psychologist Margaret Rioch has led many group meetings based on the Tavistock Group Relations Conference in which participants experience at firsthand the power of authority-dependency relationships. She describes the participants' uncanny feeling as they realize how many of their own actions have been performed at the behest of the group's unconscious intentions:

> The sense of having a will of one's own, of being free to make one's own choice, disappears, and the individual experiences himself as a marionette pulled by the strings of the group or as being a channel through which the group pours its energy and expresses itself. . . . The converse of the marionette phenomenon also occurs, especially in large groups, when an individual experiences himself as able to do anything with the group that he likes, sometimes so much so that he believes he is the group. This is often accompanied by a pseudo-religious fervor which carries the individual away into a grandiose sense of power. And this, too, is uncanny. . . . These two experiences, the sense of being all-powerful and the feeling of being a marionette, although they appear to be opposite, are essentially two sides of the same coin.[34]

Anyone who observes their own behavior will find many instances of compliance with one group or another. Furthermore, compliance becomes easier when we associate only with those who share our point of view. Then, hardly noticed, our window on reality may become so narrow that we cannot see the world, though we think we do.

4   Dependence on a Leader

ALL GROUPS HAVE LEADERS, and the primary family group is no exception. Whether the leader is formally recognized or not, someone makes the decisions and someone leads while the rest follow. The first leader we encounter is most likely to be a parent, usually our mother, the one who gives or withholds food, affection, praise, and security. Later, the father and/or other family members may take similar dominant positions in our life. Biological survival requires that we become adept at pleasing these powerful people, so as children we try to win their love and care, to avoid their wrath, and control their comings and goings as best we can. As adults, we bring to other groups the attitudes and behaviors we learned so early, directing them toward new leaders who, in the psychological sense at least, stand above us. A cult leader exploits this tendency.

It is customary to think of cult leaders as powerful personalities who inspire, even hypnotize their audiences. Charismatic leaders from Mahatma Gandhi to Adolf Hitler have been described this way. But a cult leader need not be that impressive. Alex Monroe was cerebral, his discourses boring; he was intelligent but not inspiring. He developed power by distorting his followers' idealism, dividing their loyalties, using flattery, threats, and spurious logic to defeat objections and rationalize his demands. However, one particular characteristic links Alex with other cult leaders of greater charisma—he was authoritarian.

Authoritarians emphasize obedience, loyalty, and the suppression of criticism. In the groups they lead, hierarchies of rank are emphasized and autonomy discouraged. (Sometimes such a leader takes a benign, "loving," tolerant position, but allows his or her lieutenants to enforce an authoritarian regime.)

Authoritarian leaders, especially, draw power from the dependency fantasy, from the individual's wish for an idealized parent. If we are sophisticated, we may reject, criticize, or look down on any public leader, but the wish remains, engendering seldom-noticed fantasies of someone (or something) who observes our behavior and rewards or punishes. It is not surprising that under certain conditions skepticism may be overthrown and conversion occur—as in the case of a prominent 1960s radical who one day called a meeting and dismayed his admirers by announcing that he had become a follower of an Indian guru.

MAKING OURSELVES SMALL

In our society, the tendency to look up to others while feeling small oneself is expressed in the enormous number of celebrities that clutter our minds. Statespersons, movie stars, sports figures, socialites, and the super-rich are given larger-than-life status by television and movies, by newspapers and magazines, all of which cater to this fantasy. (Sports are instructive to me, personally, in demonstrating how much I have embraced those images. Having watched football mainly on television, I have been shocked to go to a stadium and see how small the actual football field is and how mundane, ordinary, and un-godlike the players are when not projected on a television screen.)

Our predilection for inequality has even more prosaic expressions. Friends and patients alike remark that they do not feel now as they imagined their parents felt and as they still imagine "adults" feel. This misperception tends to isolate the aged. One evening, waiting for a table at a restaurant, I sat in the anteroom surrounded by gray-haired men and women, also waiting. I was struck by a sudden realization that these "oldsters" looked out at the world with the same youthful consciousness that I had. With that perception, the sense of separation from them that I had been feeling disappeared. I believe that "ageism" is not just fear of growing old, but also reveals the hidden wish to maintain a child's parental world.

THE USE AND ABUSE OF HIERARCHIES

We can trace our susceptibility to authoritarian leaders to the family structure, but in doing so we should not forget that the authoritarian character of the family is both functional and appropriate. Within the family parents and other elders are in fact superior in knowledge, experience, and strength to the children who depend on them for protection and satisfaction of needs. That parents command and children obey is realistic because of the large discrepancy in their respective capacities.

In a healthy family, as children mature and become more responsible and capable, the hierarchical, authoritarian structure moderates and becomes more democratic. Children are given appropriate responsibility and choice, which acts to reward competence and stimulate further growth. Eventually, the child's relationship to the parent reaches eye level psychologically as well as physically. This eye-level perspective is the hallmark of the mature adult. Such a perspective does not imply a denial of another's superior ability and knowledge; rather, feelings of appreciation and respect replace fear, awe, and dependency.

Just as the mature parent welcomes the child's ascent to equality and supports his or her maturation, the mature leader can and should exercise a similar function, according subordinates increasing responsibility, choice, and authority as they become capable. If this does not take place, subordinates remain in the position of children while the leader plays out the role of omnipotent parent. Thus, the key issue is not the strength of the leader, but the development or suppression of autonomy.

From this point of view, a hierarchical structure is not inherently bad; it can contribute to learning and is necessary when real differences in capacity exist. Furthermore, groups usually require a hierarchy for efficient performance of tasks. But a truly authoritarian leader is repressive and regressive.

LOOKING FOR LEADERS

The structure of cults is basically authoritarian; obedience and hierarchical power tend to take precedence over truth and conscience when they conflict, which they often do. Unfortunately, certain psychological benefits can make authoritarian groups very attractive—they provide the opportunity to feel protected and cared for. As noted earlier, the wish for parents does not disappear, but just goes underground when we become adults.

Mainstream politics provides many examples. Often, the key to a politician's popularity is the capacity to present the image of a strong, good parent, to convey an optimistic, sincere self-confidence, to communicate belief in a golden future. Apparent self-confidence and freedom from doubt are characteristics of all successful cult leaders because these postures resonate so strongly with the universal fantasy of a powerful, benign father or mother who will remove all difficulties and reassure the frightened child. As was widely remarked during Ronald Reagan's presidency, the capacity to evoke this image provides a leader with a "Teflon coating." Unpleasant, discordant facts about the leader are pushed aside to preserve the good feelings he or she can arouse. The back seat of the car exerts a strong pull.

As adults most of us leave the conduct of public affairs to others whom we prefer to believe are superior in some way because to do so is less anxiety-producing. The reality may be quite different.

A poignant comment on this situation comes from an enterprising journalist, Craig Karpel, who gained access to the 1980 Bilderberg Meeting, held at Aachen, Germany.[1] This exclusive, little-publicized summit conference of the West's power elite gathers every year to deal with whatever urgent problems face the United States and Western Europe.

As Karpel points out, if the world were secretly run by someone or something, it would be the Bilderberg group. This particular meeting included David Rockefeller, Henry Kissinger, McGeorge Bundy, Helmut Kohl, Helmut Schmidt, Lord Home, and a host of others comprising a hundred influential leaders in the fields of government, banking, publications, and industry from the various countries of the Western Alliance. The 1980 meeting took place at the beginning of a deep rift in European-American relations occasioned by Jimmy Carter's requests for sanctions against Iran and retaliation against the Soviet Union for the invasion of Afghanistan. There was also the matter of 16,000 Warsaw Pact tanks poised at the border of West Germany. The agenda for the meeting was entitled "America and Europe—Past, Present, and Future." Expecting that the men who ran things would plan a stealthy strategy of manipulation and control, dictating the future, Karpel was disappointed:

> One might imagine that the goal of Bilderberg must secretly be to attempt to shape future events and seek to profit from them. But in practice the purpose of the meetings is to assess what has already happened and to figure out how best to respond to it, with a view to hanging on to past gains.

Karpel concluded that the participants were not leaders, but managers devoted to stability and self-preservation. He concluded:

> It is not inherently sinister to convene an assembly of wise men, led by those whom the wise believe to be the wisest. But one feels a certain queasiness when, like Dorothy's little dog, Toto, one pulls aside the curtain and discovers that wizards haven't the slightest idea what to do. To insinuate oneself into such company, and to return then to the realm of roller disco and headphone radios, is like slipping up the spiral stairway of a transoceanic 747 and into the cockpit only to discover that there is no one there. The night is dark. A howling storm lies ahead. You descend to the main cabin. The dinner service has been concluded. A number of passengers are noisily airing petty complaints. The lights dim. The movie is about to begin . . .

And so the secret, the hideous grisly secret of Bilderberg is revealed. There's nobody at the controls, folks. We're flying blind. Let's hope there's foam on the runway, friends and neighbors, 'cause we're coming in on a wing and a prayer.[2]

The driver's seat is empty, the parents have gone. But who wants to know?

THE FANTASY LEADER

Looking up to a leader may be the result of a need to maintain a fantasy of the leader's superiority. Ronald Reagan was particularly attuned to fantasy's attractiveness to the public. James Barber, professor of political science at Duke University, commented in the *New York Times*:

> President Reagan's indifference to reality is hardly news. His criterion of validity is drama, not empiricism. As David Stockman, Director of the Office of Management and Budget, once summed up the White House system: "Every time one fantasy doesn't work they try another one." Mr. Reagan, told by a reporter that one of his favorite, endlessly repeated anecdotes—how a black hero at Pearl Harbor ended segregation in the armed forces—was total fiction, replied: "I remember the scene. . . . It was very powerful." What matters to him is the grace and theatrical force of a performance; as a lifelong practitioner of illusion, he is in no way embarrassed by its victory over the facts.[3]

As Barber goes on to note, the contradictions ignored by the public are striking indeed. Advocating law and order at home, Reagan violated international law and order by mining Nicaragua's waters. He blithely hailed dictators as "friends of democracy" and compared the Nicaraguan contras to the founding fathers of the United States. He secretly sold arms to a terrorist nation and lied about it when the story first broke. In the "Baby Jane Doe" case, the Reagan administration tried to force hospitals to care for hopelessly defective infants while cutting the federal funds hospitals would need to provide such special services. Similarly, Reagan opposed abortion and at the same time endeavored to slash the budgets of agencies that would provide care for unwanted infants. It didn't seem to matter. People regarded President Reagan as a nice guy, warm-hearted, sincere. He survived the Iran-contra debacle.

While Reagan's supporters ignored many of these contradictions to preserve the fantasy, his opponents erred in making Reagan a "bad father." Assigning him an evil capacity and intent, they often didn't consider that in believing his own fictions, willfully ignoring facts, rationalizing, accepting the reassurances of the friends who surrounded him, and preferring agreeable fantasies to disagreeable facts, Reagan behaved much like the rest of us. He didn't fool the public, he was the public, as other popular presidents before him have been. Those who hated him and those who loved him saw Reagan magnified, larger than themselves, and resisted an eye-level view.

Although Reagan has provided a particularly startling case of wishes dominating facts, the same process takes place in America with every president. And woe to him who falls from grace. It is interesting that the principal charge against Jimmy Carter was that he failed to provide leadership; yet he led brilliantly at Camp David. However, Carter did not appear decisive, confident, protective, optimistic; he was not, as one young woman put it about Ronald Reagan, "the father I always wanted." Jimmy Carter proved ordinary, like us, and I believe this was a major reason why voters felt he had to be replaced.

A leader's role is more complex than it might appear. As powerful as he or she might seem, a leader is also the captive of the group and may not fail the group's expectation or waver on the pedestal. If a leader does, the group may reject him. And so the eminence initially sought by the leader can become a prison; the tyrant is tyrannized. Leader and follower alike to some degree enact a dependency fantasy that requires an all-powerful parent who protects and rewards and a group of children who have no responsibilities other than obedience. The leader, as much as the group members, wishes to believe that an omnipotent, perfect parent is possible. And when a person assumes the mantle, he or she participates in the fantasy as faithfully as does the follower.

Yet it *is* still a fantasy. Margaret Rioch comments that:

. . . we do indeed long for a shepherd who will guide us into green and safe pastures. The trouble with this simile, when applied to human beings, is that the shepherd is another sheep. He may be dressed up in a long cloak and accompanied by a tall staff with a crook on the end of it or by other formidable symbols of high office. But underneath the cloak is one of the sheep, and not, alas, a member of a more intelligent and more far-seeing species. But the wish, and sometimes, the need, for a leader is so strong that it is almost always possible for one of the sheep to play the role of shepherd of the flock.[4]

THE LEADER'S FANTASY

Most people realize the danger a leader can pose; they have read of Jonestown and they know of the crimes of Stalin, Hitler, Mao Tse-tung, and Pol Pot. The precariousness and danger of the leader role for the leader is not so well known, although it is illustrated by the face of many who have headed New Age religious and utopian groups.

For Alex Monroe, leader of the Life Force movement, the need to maintain the status of a superior, omnipotent being was a key factor. Carried away by grandiose wishes, Alex expanded his activities, publishing an ambitious magazine, and establishing multiple training centers. At the same time, he was unwilling to share his power; he had to supervise and decide everything. Alex could not manage all these tasks, and he dealt with his failure by projecting blame on everyone; as a consequence, his paranoid thinking accelerated. It should be noted that his followers supported this process because they chose to overlook the contradictions between the mystical teachings he espoused and the dishonest, cruel behavior he—and they—engaged in. For his followers, to recognize what was actually taking place would have been to cease to believe in Alex as a powerful, wise parent and themselves as his disciples/children pursuing an ennobling, special path. Neither Alex nor the group wished to give up the fantasy.

A study of history reveals numerous leaders overreaching themselves, becoming inflated with an omnipotent dream they share with their followers. Perhaps because of the behavior of their emperors, the ancient Romans had an awareness of the problem of grandiosity. As a victorious general on his day of triumph rode past the cheering crowds, leading a long procession of soldiers, captured slaves, and booty, a man would stand behind him in the chariot continually whispering, "Remember, you are mortal."

It is hard for a leader to remember that he or she is mortal when followers wish for a divinity, when they attribute to the leader the qualities of a superparent. In addition, the leader finds that he or she can wield enormous influence over group members through the gratification he or she can provide or withhold. That gratification is seen in its most intense form as "bliss," which in this context can be interpreted as the joy that springs up when an adult becomes a child once again. How wonderful to relinquish all choice and decision, to be secure in the belief that the superparent will take care of everything. When, at the same time, this regression is said to be for the good of the human race, to help bring about the salvation of the world, then the bliss is complete because it seems noble as well.

WHEN FACTS DON'T COUNT

Of course, it takes some doing to maintain the fantasy of riding in the back seat of the car. Frequently, I find that a patient has refused to exercise his or her full strength, fearing the loss of a feeling of protection, of being watched over by a parental force (even a cruel one) that stands between him or her and an imagined chaos. This tendency is widespread.

When a leader's actions conflict with the group's principles, standards, or values, followers may twist words and meanings to reduce cognitive dissonance and maintain the fantasy. According to published accounts, one well-known Eastern guru with a propensity for drunkenness became angered at a visiting couple who had withdrawn from a wild party (held during a retreat) and secluded themselves in their room, refusing his commands to appear. He ordered his guards to bring them by force—which they did, breaking down the door and engaging the man in a fight during which he wielded broken glass as a weapon, wounding one of the guards. The couple was finally brought to stand before the guru, who then ordered that they be stripped naked. The woman and man were thrown to the floor and their clothes torn off. The woman called for help but only one onlooker came to their defense (and he was struck). The nude couple was then brought to stand before the guru. Shortly thereafter, everyone at the party stripped. The guru's actions were later justified by a follower: ". . . vajrayana teachings are ruthless; compassion takes many forms."[5]

Calling the drunken guru's behavior compassion is an example of what George Orwell, in *1984*, called double-speak, manipulating the abstractions of language to suggest a meaning and value opposite to the real situation. This is one way discrepancies between group fantasies and actual behavior can be painted over.

The power of the dependency fantasy is underscored in the case cited above by the fact that the abused couple chose to stay on for the conclusion of the retreat. The man explained, "We'd come to study the whole course; we'd taken it (as he [the guru] knew) seriously; we wanted to finish what we'd begun, and not be scared off. The last lap, about to begin, was the famous Tantric teachings."[6]

In such extreme cases, the individual's perception has to be narrowed and critical thinking suppressed. Groups have effective means of doing this. As in Clara Robinson's case, if a group member voices objections or criticism, he or she may be attacked as ignorant, unworthy, selfish, elitist—whatever term is used to define badness. Groups, as well as leaders, may punish dissent or deviation when maintenance of the superparent fantasy requires that no imperfections be revealed lest the whole structure be put in jeopardy. Seldom does anyone stand behind the leader to whisper, "Remember, you are mortal."

In a cult the leader is accepted as having special powers and/or semidivine status which places him or her outside the behavior norms of the ordinary person. As we have seen, similar exemption from the rules and the accompanying claim to infallibility enables many a leader to perform unethical acts that would otherwise not be countenanced. In ordinary life traces of this dynamic can be seen, although the situation is seldom as stark as in extreme cults.

When facts become impossible to ignore, the leader is dethroned; but all too often the dependency fantasy continues; a new "parent" is found.

We find examples of the abuses of the role of leader in recent political history. Richard Nixon's handling of the Watergate break-in suggests that being president had eroded his judgment, encouraged grandiosity, and blinded him with the righteousness that arises easily in powerful leaders when they are criticized and challenged. For absolute rulers the danger is even worse; witness the career of Idi Amin, who ended up rivaling Caligula in the bloody, paranoid expressions of his vanity and fear.

THE DRAW OF IDEALISM

We have seen how the idealism of Hugh and Clara was used as a lever to break their ties with family members and to justify unethical, harmful actions. Idealism can be exploited as a source of a leader's power; he or she need only inspire and mobilize the readiness for self-sacrifice that exists within many people.

In the business world, the importance of generating fervor was noted by Thomas Peters and Robert Waterman, Jr., in their studies of "excellent" companies. They found that "transforming leadership" played a crucial role in the history of outstanding corporations; charismatic leaders stirred the emotions of their employees so as to instill a sense of elevated purpose, fulfilling the crucial human need for meaning and purpose.

Sometimes the meaning may not seem very profound to an outside observer. Charles Edward Wilson, president of General Electric from 1940 to 1950, created a strong impression on Reginald Jones (who himself later became president of the company):

> I still remember Charlie Wilson, the very epitome of the inspirational leader. He told us, in the Town Hall, how Westinghouse planned to surpass us in sales and earnings. 'They should live so long!' he roared. 'Their grandchildren should live so long.' And then he got us out behind the marching band, and they led us out to the flagpole play-

ing 'Onward Christian Soldiers.' At that moment, I would have followed him anywhere on earth—and beyond if necessary.[7]

Even if the summons is for political or economic goals rather than religious ones, the energies mobilized will be the same and the final result is declared to be for the greater good, creating paradise on earth, saving the world. What matters is that people's deepest desires for the Good be mobilized. That is why the most effective leaders inspire rather than overpower. This was the conclusion of a study of audience reactions to a charismatic leader:

> They were apparently strengthened and uplifted by the experience; they felt more powerful, rather than less powerful or submissive. This suggests that the traditional way of explaining the influence of a leader on his followers has not been entirely correct. He does not force them to submit and follow him by the sheer overwhelming magic of his personality and persuasive powers . . . he is influential by strengthening and inspiriting his audience.[8]

Anyone who has watched films of Hitler's speeches and the crowds' reactions would agree. Hitler, transformed by his own fantasies, brought his audience's fantasies and wishes to life, made them seem possible. He whipped his listeners to intoxicating heights of emotion, restoring significance to their lives, asking for sacrifices.

Most of us need to feel that our lives have meaning and purpose, that we are special and arc living in a way that is consonant with our ideals. And it is not only the young who long to live idealistically, older people who have led practical lives and have accepted the necessity of compromising their ideals may respond with great commitment if offered the opportunity to sacrifice for a good cause. This appeal to the perception of a larger reality, to unsatisfied idealism and the wish for meaning can be very powerful, and it can be put to good or bad use. As will be described in detail later on, the terrorist group al Qaeda makes primary use of this appeal to recruit and train its members.

The business world too is not immune from the seduction of the leader as fantasy parent.

UP AND DOWN THE CORPORATE LADDER

Authoritarian leadership tends to become established in large corporations where power has become overly centralized. Harold Geneen, who ran ITT like a potentate, knows whereof he speaks: "The authority vested in the chief executive of a large company is so great, so complete, and the demands made upon his time are so consuming, that most chief executives slip into authoritarian roles without realizing that the process is going on."[9]

John De Lorean, former General Motors executive, describes the increase in authoritarianism at General Motors in the years following the departure of Alfred Sloan, who had been chairman of the board:

> I watched GM's operations slowly become centralized. The divisions gradually were stripped of their decision-making power. . . . The guiding corporate precept of centralized policymaking and decentralized decision making was totally and purposefully ignored. . . . There was no system of checks and balances. The divisions reported to The Fourteenth Floor. But The Fourteenth Floor reported only to itself.[10]

The authoritarian attitude results in an emphasis on punishment and the manifestation of power by saying No. The veto is safer and more impressive than granting permission. Although innovation and creativity may be given lip service, even insignificant mistakes are usually punished despite their being the inevitable price of developing a new approach or a new product.[11]

Peters and Waterman, Jr., in reviewing the problem, came to the conclusion that this behavior reflects the same superior/inferior perspective that Erich Fromm emphasized in his study of authoritarian political behavior.[12] "Central to the whole notion . . . is the superior/subordinate relationship, the idea of manager as 'boss,' and the corollary that orders will be issued and followed. The threat of punishment is the principle implied power that underlies it all."[13]

The hierarchical emphasis is underlined by corporate class distinctions. The executive washroom, the special dining room for upper management, superior furnishings, and more space are all indicators of a higher position. Indeed, the top executives usually will be found on the highest floor. This institutionalization of the upward gaze is accepted almost everywhere and seldom questioned any more than is the assumption of parents having the largest bedroom in the home, a separate bathroom, and other special prerogatives.

Even when the chief executive officer wishes to make the organization less authoritarian, the task is not easy. Cornelle Meier, former CEO for Kaiser Aluminum recalls a lesson he learned when his corporation began to decentralize decision-making:

> As we started giving more authority to our operating divisions an interesting thing happened . . . all of the managers working for me felt that they should have a lot more authority in their decision-making: capital spending, personnel moves—what have you. That wasn't a surprise. What was a surprise was that nearly all of them felt that the people working for them shouldn't have more authority! . . . They wanted a lot more authority but they didn't want to give that authority away.[14]

Nor did they wish to give up the symbols of elevated status they had acquired as part of the superior/inferior authoritarian world.

UNINTENDED CONSEQUENCES OF POWER

The chief executive officer of a large corporation does not usually claim divine attributes. However, the CEO's power to hire, fire, reward, and punish is very great and in the hands of an authoritarian personality this power can result in a suppression of critical thinking within the corporation and a mindless conformity and fawning support for whatever the CEO believes and decides to do. Sometimes this behavior extends to a slavish copying of the style of dress and behavior of the boss. In his book, *The Fanciest Dive,* Christopher Byron gives an amusing description of the antics that took place at Time, Inc. when a new boss, Richard Munro, entered the scene:

> No sooner did word spread that the company's new president ate breakfast early most mornings at the Dorset Hotel on West Fifty-

fourth Street than numerous subordinates began doing the same. It was there, one hot September morning in 1982 that Munro, having breakfast, stood up and removed his suit jacket to be more comfortable; all around the room Time Inc. executives promptly rose and did the same. . . . And when Munro took to carrying a red bandana with a corner flapping loosely from his hip pocket, the corridors of the Big House were soon ablaze with red bandanas waving jauntily from the hip pockets of hopeful executives.[15]

Like similar leaders everywhere, authoritarian executives can easily end up valuing the conformity, loyalty, obedience, and subservience of subordinates more than actual performance. A boss wants to trust his or her subordinates, to count on their loyalty, to know they fit in and will not cause trouble. Subordinates who conform to the boss's own style of dress and behavior evoke in him a sense of support and comfort. The boss feels he knows where his subordinates stand and can rely on them to perform as he would in unsupervised situations. In turn, the employees know that salaries, promotion, and assignments within the company lie in the hands of their boss. When obedience, loyalty, and conformity matter more than performance, cult-like behavior takes place all along the hierarchy. Secrecy about salaries, competition for the boss's favor, and fear of being left behind can create an atmosphere reminiscent of that which occurred in Life Force. One manager described:

> A big fear complex that operates within GPI because there are so many people who are, or will, or might be your boss, or might be or do have an influence on you one way or the other. The fear syndrome keeps you from speaking up and it works in the compensation area as well. While you may know your salary, obviously more money is at the whimsical beck and call of your boss and his boss and a few other people perhaps.[16]

SUBMISSION AND SECURITY

In more recent years, the CEO has gained almost mythical status as the charismatic leader who will take a company to new heights, or save it from its declining fortunes. This wish/belief has been accompanied by a grotesque salary structure. As reported by Rakesh Khurana, assistant professor of business administration at Harvard, in 1981, the average pay of a CEO of large business was $1,083,000. By 2001, it averaged $10,457,800. The average worker's pay was $25,466. The compensation awarded celebrity CEOs is said to reflect their great effect on a company's success. But Khurana's research found no such stable effect. Rewards seem independent of actual performance. He provides an anecdote reported by *Business Week,* pertaining to AT&T, in which at a board meeting in December 2000, CEO Mike Armstrong was asked to wait outside while the board reviewed his performance. In that year AT&T had cut its dividend for the first time in its history and its stock price had fallen from sixty dollars a share to eighteen dollars. When Mike Freeman returned an hour later, "the board exploded with a standing ovation." Khurana attributes this situation to the quest for charismatic leadership. As summarized by *Harvard Magazine* editor Craig Lambert:

> Charismatic leadership, which grows from a personal magnetism that inspires devotion, reaches its apotheosis in religious cults. Its ascendance in corporate life is 'a throwback to an earlier form of authority that proved to be very unstable.' . . . The atavistic corporate quest for charismatic CEOs, with its deference to the personality and vision of a particular individual comes bundled with risks of abuse, misconduct, and incompetence. The results are now spread before us, and their name is not Legion, but Enron.[17]

What is a god if not a supreme authority? In religions the world over, the devout acknowledge their god's divine wisdom, mercy, and awesome power; they pray for protection, forgiveness, and benefits. Even in Buddhism, whose founder declared that notions of gods and heavens were illusions, most believers bow to a Buddha idol with all the expectations found in theistic religions.

Few people take seriously the injunctions of mystics against seeking to understand the Ultimate via familiar images. Typical of such an injunction is the statement of Saint John of the Cross:

That inward wisdom is so simple, so general and so spiritual that it has not entered into the understanding enwrapped or clad in any form or image subject to sense, it follows that sense and imagination (as it has not entered through them nor has taken their form and color) cannot account for it or imagine, so as to say anything concerning it, although the soul be clearly aware that it is experiencing and partaking of that rare and delectable wisdom.[18]

Saint John maintained that knowledge of God cannot be expressed in terms of this world, cannot be articulated by using the images and concepts of everyday life: family, mother, father, children, reward, punishment. Similar statements about the unknowability of the Godhead have been made by mystics of widely differing cultures throughout history. They are very consistent. Nevertheless, formal religions tend to use the familiar relationship of parent and child as the model for a human being's relationship to the divine. This model inevitably creates cult dynamics in religious organizations. In part, the problem arises because the founding mystics of the theistic religions, in their attempts to communicate the ineffable, made use of the concept of God the Father, the supreme parent, although only as a metaphor. However, their listeners took the meaning literally. Thus, religions end up teaching, be good (obey God's wishes) and you will be rewarded (enter Heaven or nirvana); if you are bad (disobey God), you will be punished (with Hell or reincarnation).

The dependency wish usually requires tangible authority figures and they are seldom in short supply. Mohammed abolished the priesthood but equivalent ecclesiastical officials, the mullahs, arose after his death and in some areas, such as Iran (now a theocracy), the chief mullah rules with more authority than the present day Pope. Another example is provided by Hinduism. Although the Upanishads preach the oneness of all being, the Brahmin priests whose function it is to transmit Hindu teaching have maintained the caste system and their superior status within it. It took all the power of Gandhi to begin to crack the caste barriers that discriminated against the untouchables of India.

Theistic religions, such as Christianity, Judaism, or Islam, are intrinsically authoritarian, expressing the belief in God as a Supreme Being who transcends the material world, is infinitely superior to human beings, and to whom we owe obedience. God's absolute superiority in power, goodness, and knowledge may be used by religious leaders to justify their own authority and to legitimize their demands for submission. For the most part, theistic religions teach that compliance with God's will, coupled with an appropriately humble attitude, will be rewarded by protection and help for the supplicant: that pride (putting oneself at eye level with God) is a sin and submission a virtue. The greater the emphasis on the supreme god (the superparent) versus the inferior follower (the child), the more the stage is set for cult behavior in any religion, orthodox or not.

Thus, as in any authoritarian system, the basic perspective of most religious groups is one of superior/inferior relationships; as obedience is the prime virtue in all authoritarian systems, so obedience to God's commandments is a prime virtue in theistic religions. This is espoused most rigidly by fundamentalists, those who believe in the literal, inerrant truth of the Bible, the Koran, or any other religious text. Reverend Jerry Falwell puts the matter most unequivocally: "We must be obedient to the Word of God. Obedient. Whatsoever He sayeth unto you, do it! That's all there is to it! Find out what God is saying to you and obey Him. Obey the Lord. Obedience!" [19]

Of course, the critical issue is not obedience, per se, but why we are obedient and to what or to whom. Blind obedience leads to totalitarianism, refusal to obey anything leads to chaos. Free will (as distinguished from impulsivity) combines obedience with choice; it is "the experience of being the author of the law you obey." [20] Being the author means to choose the values expressed in the law, to freely assent to them based on one's judgment, experience, and sense of the Good.

The best religious leaders teach that a truly spiritual choice is an expression of one's self and not an expression of fear (of punishment), or greed (for reward), or vanity (being one of the chosen few). A story from the Sufic tradition, here told by Idries Shah, addresses this issue:

THREE REASONS

There was once a powerful conqueror who had become emperor of a vast territory peopled by representatives of several beliefs.

His counselors said, "Great king, a deputation of thinkers and priests from each persuasion, is awaiting audience. Each hopes to convert you to the way of thinking of his school. We are in a quandary, because we cannot advise you to accept the ideology of one part, since it would alienate the goodwill of all the rest."

The king, for his part, said, "Neither is it fitting that a king should adopt beliefs for political reasons, and without thought for his own higher dignity and well-being."

The discussions continued for several hours, until a wise dervish, who had attached himself to the king's retinue many months before and had been silent ever since, stepped forward.

"Majesty," he said, "I am prepared to advise a course in which the interests of all parties will be safeguarded. The applicants will be abashed, the courtiers will be relieved of their anxiety to find a solution, the king will be able to retain his reputation for wisdom, and nobody will be able to say that he holds sway over the king's thoughts."

The dervish whispered his formula into the royal ear, and the king called the deputation to enter the throne-room.

Receiving the clerics and thinkers with all courtesy, the king said to them:

"I shall hear first of all the arguments of those among you who do not say 'Believe or you are in peril'; or 'Believe because it will give you happiness', or 'Adopt my beliefs because you are a great king.'"

The applicants dispersed in confusion.[21]

Reprinted by permission from The Way of the Sufi
by Idries Shah (Octagon Press Ltd., London)

Although a person may be drawn to a religion through the wish to find meaning and purpose, to serve God and humanity, religious organizations all too often fail to avoid stimulating fear, greed, or vanity in recruiting members. Consequently, the obedience commanded tends to evoke the attitude of the child toward its parent. Obedience is certainly necessary for certain kinds of learning and development, and has a definite function in religious instruction, but great religious teachers agree that the highest obedience is to the religion's essence.

Obedience to the literal scriptures, to the form rather than the essence, opens the door to cult processes. This problem of form taking precedence over content is one that plagues all religions and is defined as idolatry. Anything can be idolized, including rules and rituals, and the resulting behavior may contradict the values that the religion espouses. A Benedictine prioress reflected on the reversal of priorities that marked religious life during her early years with the order:

> Formalism and legalism had completely replaced either spiritual direction or blessing. Every day life got smaller. Religious life had become the celebration of the trivial. While McCarthyism raged, I was told to guard myself from spiritual distraction by not listening to the news. While Martin Luther King began black sit-ins of white lunch counters in a country that routinely lynched blacks, I believed it when they said that had nothing to do with religious life and concentrated on darning my socks, a real sign of poverty, I was told.[22]

When a religion's texts are regarded as literally true and infallible, a likely next step is that the leader's interpretation becomes what is true and sacred. Then a member's obedience is transferred to the priest, rabbi, mullah, or minister; this is the lowest level of obedience, most likely to lead to overt cult behavior. Reverend R. G. Puckett, the Baptist evangelist who heads Americans United, warned of this development taking place in American Christian fundamentalist churches:

> The church is centered in the pastor. He is the authority, the ruling force. Falwell, Robison, Robertson, all the rest—these are personality cults. People follow the person, the pastor, not Jesus Christ. He may say he is not telling anyone how to vote or how to live, but the very climate and mentality of the whole church says: what the pastor wants is what we do.[23]

Such preachers do not claim divinity, only that God speaks to them, inspires them, guides them. That claim may be quite enough to demand complete obedience and to brand disagreement with their views and wishes as a sign that the defiant member is lost to salvation.

Religious leaders may be as attracted to the security of certainty and surrender as are their followers. Many really believe they are commanded by God, that they have become instruments of his will, and that their pronouncements are beyond error. Others with less exalted views of themselves nevertheless succumb to the lure of certainty and rightness. From a priest who has faced the shortcomings of his church we have an eloquent testimony to that attraction:

> I do not [now] live without worry or responsible concern. In fact, I have never felt so responsible since I discovered that the Church cannot absorb my conscience, nor replace my mind. Life was easier when I knew where everything fit, when I could lose myself in the structure of a massive organization. There heaven and hell were governed by careful laws. There God's friendship was certain and manageable, and I was satisfied when I kept the Church's rules.[24]

Liz Harris, writing in the *New Yorker,* contrasted her own state of uncertainty with the security of the Hasidic world:

> I envied them their sureness and the sheer weight it gave them. I had, of course, my family, my friends, my work, and the various pleasures that came my way, but spiritually I felt as if I floated weightlessly in the universe. The Hasidim had a world without time, eternal life, and the extraordinary sense that everything they did counted.[25]

THE REWARDS OF SURRENDER

Surrender is a basic feature of the spiritual life. As an acceptance of selfless goals in place of self-centeredness, it is something most recognize as inherently desirable. Yet the call to surrender can become a tool for manipulation and control when critical judgment is set aside. As we have seen earlier, Clara Robinson was exhorted to give up her concern for her child and surrender to Life Force's greater spiritual task as set forth by Alex Monroe. Her reluctance to do so was defined as selfishness. Barbara Underwood, a former Moonie, described similar coercion in the Unification Church,[26] and total surrender is called for by fundamentalist preachers and organizations such as the Campus Crusade. Bill Bright, writing in *Jesus and the Intellectual* makes it quite explicit: "The secret is surrender. Commitment to Christ involves the surrender of the intellect, the emotions and the will—the total person."[27]

There is no place in such groups for reasoned, independent judgment; no free will, no responsible choice, only literal adherence to sacred text as selected and interpreted by the church leader or organization. With surrender, the authority of the leader is maximized, the follower feels relieved of uncertainty and choice and can then experience the "bliss" of someone who has "returned home."

THE CULT CONTINUUM

Since most of the examples I have cited are from the fundamentalist and conservative wings of established religions, some readers may feel my conclusions do not apply to them because they are involved in less doctrinaire, more moderate, more sophisticated beliefs and practices. I would respond that it is a matter of degree and that each person needs to assess the extent to which cult behavior and the dependency fantasy are operative in his or her religious life.

I believe that such awareness is of particular importance because the goal of religion should be to facilitate the direct experience of the spiritual dimension. Although human beings carry within them the potential for regressive dependency, they also contain the potential for the intuition of the spiritual—that perception, however dim, of something that transcends the reality accessible to the senses and ordinary thought. This intuition is universal and can be very powerful.[28]

Indeed, mystics claim that spiritual development consists of strengthening that inborn intuitive capacity, permitting one to "know" the larger reality called Truth, God, Original Mind, Brahma—whatever name may be invoked.[29] Assuming the existence of that perceptual capacity, latent in everyone, the question arises of the effect of cult-like behavior on one's capacity to experience the spiritual.

Study of the mystical literature of many religions reveals all these traditions to be in agreement that to develop the ability to perceive God or Truth, one must shift from a self-centered orientation to serving the underlying reality. This service must be without concern for personal gain; basic intentions must change. There can be no cheating on this one because motivation determines the form of consciousness. You cannot grasp the spiritual world as you can the material since a "grasping" mind is necessarily focused on discrete objects and cannot encompass a world of connectedness, of unity. It is for this reason—a functional, not a moral reason—that mystics assert that no matter what you may say or do, no matter how you may appear, if your underlying intention is self-centered, perception of Truth or God is impossible. The necessary shift in motivation takes time, effort, and skillful guidance. To "repent and believe" is not enough.

An organization that enhances selfish intentions is at cross purposes with spiritual development; it is anti-spiritual.[30] To stimulate fear of punishment, greed for reward, or vanity at being among the saved versus the damned, is to stimulate a self-centered orientation. These powerful motivations are not in the service of spiritual development. This is why one saint declared:

> O Lord!
> If I worship you from fear of hell, cast me into hell.
> If I worship you from desire for paradise, deny me paradise.[31]

Dependence on a leader/parent can be doubly destructive in the sphere of religion. Not only does it impair ordinary judgment and create a regressive pull on members and converts of religious groups, it prevents them from progressing beyond a self-centered orientation. This blocks the perception of the spiritual force that is the vital element within religions, a force that might otherwise enhance and guide their lives.

I do not mean to say that a religion's members may not devote themselves to actions benefiting others. To the contrary, great charity and service have been inspired by religious beliefs and administered by religious institutions throughout the centuries. Cult behavior is largely an interior problem in which form (doctrine and authority) dominates content (the experience of the Real), producing idolatry. Understanding the nature of the problem facilitates an attitude vitally different from the authoritarian. A School Sister of Notre Dame comments:

> Although as a woman religious I am identified with church institutions, in the final analysis, God, not any institution, is paramount. To associate with and to preserve any structure at the expense of serving God and humankind is idolatry. To follow God's call rather than an institutional call, if the two are in conflict, is a moral imperative. I pray always for the grace and the insight to discern God's call.[32]

Certainly, if a religious group provides us with security and identity, we will not see its cult features very readily. One's own group is thought to be above such behavior; a cult is seen as something that you yourself don't belong to. But perhaps in some ways you do. It just isn't obvious when measured against Jonestown or the Life Force Institute.

DANGERS IN PSYCHOTHERAPY

My own profession of psychiatry is not immune from cult behavior. To begin with, the psychotherapeutic situation itself encourages the emergence of a dependency relationship. In psychoanalysis and analytically oriented psychotherapy, the therapist reveals almost nothing while the patient is expected to reveal all. Since the therapist is calm, reticent, and an authority while the patient is distressed and seeking help, a parent/child feeling quickly develops. With time, the unique character of the patient's early relationship to his or her parent or parents tends to be transferred to the therapist. In fact Freud emphasized the importance of this transference in helping the patient and saw the intensification of the parent/child fantasy as a desired effect of the psychotherapeutic situation.

Nevertheless, it should be recognized that Freud intended that the patient reclaim the power he or she bestowed on the therapist. He hoped that analysis of the transference would give to the patient an eye-level perspective toward the analyst, as well as toward others. I know of no other profession or institution that has established a goal of relinquishing authority and built-in comprehensive techniques for its accomplishment. Even though the return of power takes place only imperfectly (and in some cases not at all), dedication to an eye-level relationship is a direct counter to cult-like behavior and offers hope for a more mature society.

Regrettably, the ideal may be preached but not always practiced. Psychotherapists may exploit their position in the same fashion as do cult leaders. This can take place in several ways, from automatically interpreting a patient's criticism as neurotic, dismissing any questioning as projection or acting out of the transference, to outright sexual seduction. I remember a cartoon about psychiatry with the punch line "This is the only business where the customer is always wrong."

The patient is not always wrong in his or her perceptions of the therapist. It is crucial that the therapist be able to see in what ways the patient is correct, acknowledge and support the patient's perception, and go on to investigate what the therapist's error or limitation means to the patient. Competent therapists do this, but only an ideal therapist is completely free from defensiveness and denial.

Therapists, like other leaders, often are flattered and idealized by their patients, who wish them to be omnipotent, omniscient, surrogate parents. Resisting this seduction is particularly difficult for a psychotherapist because he or she is likely to have entered the profession with the very fantasy of being an ideal parent, one who "saves" grateful patients. (In this context, the patient may represent the therapist as a child or the therapist's parent, whoever needed saving.) Having become a therapist, one may fall in with the patient's wish when it supports the savior fantasy. While the patient is not officially a follower, nor is the therapist a cult leader, the dependency needs of the former and the omnipotent fantasies of the latter can create cult-like behavior.

Actual cults may develop in therapeutic situations. Although this is rare, there have been instances of therapists who develop relationships with their patients in which they occupy the roles of colleagues, teachers, lovers, friends, and employers simultaneously. Such a violation of professional ethics and psychiatric principles is not necessarily due to substandard psychiatric training. In one study of five such "therapeutic cults," two of the leaders were psychoanalysts, members of the prestigious American Psychoanalytic Association, yet these therapeutic cults functioned almost like religious cults.[33] Although actual cult formation by psychiatrists is unusual, there are two areas where covert cult-like behavior is significant.

WORRISOME PRACTICES IN PSYCHOANALYTIC INSTITUTES

In the 1950s and 1960s, psychoanalysis was in its heyday of acceptance and power. The heads of departments of psychiatry in medical schools were usually psychoanalysts; it was assumed that the best psychiatry residents would become psychoanalysts—the second-best would have to settle for something inferior. Indeed, as a psychiatric resident, I was told that only psychoanalysis offered a patient real change, real treatment; psychotherapy was a patch-up job. (How powerfully such a consensus prevailed and affected judgment is hard to convey, even though there were abundant cases of unresolved neurotic problems among former analysands and among the training analysts themselves, and although one heard anecdotes of psychotherapy results that rivaled the best of psychoanalysis.) This assumption pervades much of the psychoanalytic literature today and I think it has had a debilitating effect on psychoanalytic thinking.

Psychoanalytic institutes, where psychoanalysis is taught, are not cults, but cult behavior does take place in them. Cult features have been so prominent that noted analysts have remarked on the similarity between psychoanalytic institutes and religious organizations. Otto Kernberg, training analyst at the Columbia University Center for Psychoanalytic Training and Research, points to features of psychoanalytic education that justify its designation as a system of religious beliefs:

The religious assertion of faith in the existence of the deity and the essentially irrational nature of such a faith are not unlike the sense of conviction about the truth of psychoanalytic theory, particularly about the unconscious. This sense of conviction is usually traced to an emotional experience connected with the discovery of the unconscious in oneself and the experience of psychological change following this discovery. In both instances a highly subjective personal experience, an emotional encounter with the unknown rather than rational analysis, constitutes the anchoring pillar of the educational program.[34]

This could be a description of Hugh and Clara Robinson's conversion to faith in life force psychology, or of the experiences of converts to the numerous new religions of the sixties and seventies. Kernberg goes on to point out further similarities:

In addition, this deeply transforming emotional experience is carried out in the context of an intense relation to another person, idealized and experienced as a spiritual guide . . . complemented by other mentors who focus on the limitations, shortcomings, mistakes, and inadequacies of the student's performance, while sustaining the assumption that they are working at a higher level, which the student must reach through ongoing self-exploration as well as learning about the formulations of the masters, in the end, the original master of the school, Freud.[35]

The analogy to religion is seconded by Jacob Arlow, a past president of the American Psychoanalytic Association, who pointed out that psychoanalytic education is unique among learned disciplines in that most of its basic texts are fifty years old. He observes that this can't be wholly explained as the debt of psychoanalysis to Freud because of a characteristic clinging to the past that marks the educational emphasis. Freud's earlier writings receives greater attention than either his later (superceding) writings or the contributions of recent analysts.[36] Arlow further notes that psychoanalytic training is experienced as a prolonged initiation rite:

During a long course of tests which the initiates undergo (personal analysis, admission to courses, first case, second case, etc., graduation), the training analysts serve the double function characteristic of all initiators. Some intimidate the candidates; others act as sponsors and guides . . . anxiety propels the candidate into effecting an identification with the aggressor; the initiate remodels himself after the image the community holds up as the ideal.[37]

The situation of the candidates is not unlike that of members of Life Force who were dependent on the good opinion of leader/therapist Alex for their graduation to the inner circle of the Center. Depending on the candidate, the effects could easily be similar in kind.

BLIND FOLLOWERS AND BLIND LEADERS

In 1961 John F. Kennedy made the disastrous decision to go ahead with a covert invasion of Cuba by anti-Castro exiles, an operation commonly referred to afterward as the Bay of Pigs. It was a spectacular failure. About a year later, when it was discovered that Russian nuclear missiles were being installed in Cuba, Kennedy was successful in bringing about their withdrawal, an operation usually called the Cuban Missile Crisis. Because the Bay of Pigs and the Cuban Missile Crisis were historic events whose decision-making processes are exceptionally well documented, I will use them to illustrate both cult behavior and the possibility of more realistic behavior at the government level.

Irving Janis, a psychologist who studied the effect of group process on presidential advisory groups, pointed to the important role of shared illusions in disasters such as the attempted invasion of Cuba. One was "the illusion of invulnerability." People believe that if their leader and everyone else think a proposal will succeed, then it will, even if it is risky and requires luck.

An air of omniscience and invulnerability is fostered by political leaders as well, in part because the public demands leaders who are forceful and confident; unwavering optimism is preferred to doubts and uncertainty. The fantasy of invulnerability is identical in cults, where it may lead to disaster. For example, an epochal celebration, brainchild of a young Indian guru, was held some years ago in Houston, Texas. With the guru's approval, his followers hired the Astrodome, expecting to fill it with thousands of people who would be drawn there to hear his message. Confidence was unbounded, no doubts were heard, as the guru was presumed infallible. Publicity and preparations were extensive and lavish, media coverage nationwide. The celestial appearance of the comet Kahoutek was interpreted as a cosmic herald of the grand event. What actually took place was a grand fiasco; although droves of the guru's followers arrived at the stadium, very few others availed themselves of the opportunity to adulate him and share in the momentous event. The monetary and public relations losses were staggering; the organization went into decline.

From the blissful, blind optimism of this guru and his followers to the arrogant overconfidence of top U.S. government officials in the Bay of Pigs advisory group was not such a large step. Robert Kennedy recalled, "It seemed that, with John Kennedy leading us and with all the talent he had assembled, *nothing could stop us.*" [38]

Arthur Schlesinger felt the same:

> One further factor no doubt influenced him [John F. Kennedy]: the enormous confidence in his own luck. Everything had broken right for him since 1956. He had won the nomination and the election against all the odds in the book. Everyone around him thought he had the Midas touch and could not lose. Despite himself, even this dispassionate and skeptical man may have been affected by the soaring euphoria of the new day.[39]

One cannot understand the phenomenon of authoritarian behavior in democratically elected presidents without appreciating the attraction for both leaders and followers of a superior/inferior, parent/child perspective.

I have a vivid memory of an incident that occurred during a Tavistock Group Relations Conference. Participants were divided into several large groups and each group was asked to relate to the other groups by appointing suitably empowered representatives. No group leaders were designated, no goals or structure provided. In the absence of authority and direction, anxiety built up rapidly. Everyone talked at once. I tried to reduce the chaos by establishing leadership. "Make me leader!" I pleaded. The group would not appoint any one to that power position. The disorganization and tension increased. Finally, I stood up; shouted, "I'm taking command!" and began appointing people to assume the functions of doorkeeper, ambassador, and so forth. The same people who would not voluntarily delegate authority now obeyed with alacrity. The conference conditions had intensified our primitive impulses and we behaved like a group of sibling children, no one willing to take the adult action of delegating power. When my discomfort drove me to take the role of dictator/parent the others readily submitted, for they were then freed of responsibility.

A parallel need—to structure a situation in terms of a child rebelling against a bad parent—was illustrated, for me, when I had to hospitalize an adolescent against his will. A state trooper arrived at my office to take him away. It was clear that the officer wanted to be compassionate and helpful. My patient would have none of this. He resisted, struggled, taunted, and provoked the trooper until the man became angry and, finally, cuffed him on the head with his open hand. Immediately, the young man became docile and accompanied him readily. It was clear to me that my patient had succeeded in his aim of making the policeman a "bad parent." Later, a teacher at the boy's school denounced this "police brutality" and was indignant when I replied that I thought the state trooper was the one who had been brutalized.

In each of these incidents, those involved refused or were unable to go beyond the child/parent relationship and insisted on an authoritarian structure. I see the compliance of the first instance and the rebelliousness of the second as two aspects of looking up at authority.

THE POWER OF A HIGHER AUTHORITY

Like most cults and formal religions, governments cite a higher principle or authority to justify their actions. (This is probably what Samuel

Johnson mocked when he said, "Patriotism is the last refuge of the scoundrel.") As Alex Monroe's lies were justified as being necessary to advance the work of saving the world, other cult leaders, tyrants, and terrorists invariably defend immoral and violent actions as serving God or truth or country or freedom.

Psychologist Stanley Milgram's research demonstrated the effectiveness of this reference to a higher authority. People from all walks of life participated as subjects in his studies. An experimenter in a gray lab coat told the subjects that the purpose of the experiment was to advance science, and then instructed them to give increasing electric shocks to a "learner" strapped into an electric chair. (Unbeknownst to the subjects, the learner was a confederate of the researchers and actually received no shocks at all.) The subjects were told that although the shocks could be extremely painful to the learner, they caused no permanent damage.

As the experiment proceeded, the learner became increasingly vocal, agitated, and desperate, and eventually screamed each time the subject shocked him. He demanded and begged to be released, expressing concern for his heart. Most subjects showed evidence of considerable stress as they were ordered to continue despite the anguished cries of pain, which they could hear from the other room. (In further experiments in which the learner was in the same room with them, the subjects could also see his tortured appearance.)

Contrary to predictions, most subjects continued to administer the electric shock right up to the supposed limit of 450 volts, labeled "Danger: Severe Shock." When the learner was in the same room 40 percent of the subjects continued to the end of the scale and even when the subject was required to force the learner's hand down onto the shock plate and hold it there against his struggles, 30 percent applied the most severe shocks possible. To appreciate these results it is important to understand that the acting of the learner was very convincing; follow-up studies confirmed that almost all the subjects believed that shocks were actually being administered and that the man was suffering severe pain.

Many of the subjects showed evidence of great stress as they complied with the experimenter's instructions. What direct pressure made the subjects continue despite their own distress at what they were doing? It consisted of the following statements, said firmly but politely by the experimenter, using as many of them as might be needed to overcome the subject's protests and concerns: "Please continue, [or] please go on," "The experiment requires that you continue," "It is absolutely essential that you continue," "You have no other choice, you must go on." There were no threats, no physical coercion, no other inducements.

Milgram came to the conclusion that in such situations people enter into what he terms an agentic state, one in which they see themselves as agents for carrying out another person's wishes. This shift from autonomous functioning to submission to a hierarchy of command is considered by Milgram to be an evolutionary development that has enabled human beings to take advantage of the benefits of being in large groups. Unfortunately, it may also lead one to administer suffering on others if it is justified by authority.[40]

> The human element behind the agencies and institutions is denied. Thus, when the experimenter says, "The experiment requires that you continue," the subject feels this to be an imperative that goes beyond any merely human command. He does not ask the seemingly obvious question, "Whose experiment? Why should the designer be served while the victim suffers?" The wishes of a man—the designer of the experiment—have become part of a schema which exerts on the subject's mind a force that transcends the personal.[41]

It is easy to see how this type of justification has led to nations' transgressing human values. In our own country after the Japanese bombed Pearl Harbor, blameless American citizens were dispossessed and forcibly moved into internment camps for the duration of the war because they were of Japanese descent. In the name of national security the fundamental values and principles of our democracy were thrust aside and great injustice done. Similarly, as a nation (and despite internal dissent), we justified our actions in Vietnam by the concept of "fighting Communist aggression" as we attempted to defoliate the forests with Agent Orange and napalmed civilians. The American government has supported—and still supports—governments whose murderous savagery and sickening use of torture equals, if not surpasses, Stalin's and, with the possible exception of genocide, rivals that of the Nazis. We are likely to be told that the national interest requires our support. Just as the experiment in Milgram's study assumed an impersonal, overriding authority, even more so does the national interest. As Noam Chomsky noted in a symposium on human rights:

> The concept of "national interest" [is] a mystification that serves to conceal the ways in which state policy is formed and executed. . . . Within a particular nation-state, some groups are sufficiently powerful to exert a major, perhaps dominant, influence over state policy and the ideological systems. Their special interests then become, in effect, "the national interest." To take again the case of Guatemala: in 1954 the United Fruit Company had an interest in blocking land reform: I did not. . . . What was "the national interest?" In practice, it was the special interest of those with the power to influence and execute state policy and to shape the basic structure of the ideological system, including the flow of information.[42]

We can understand the power of "the experiment," "the state," and "the national interest," "God's will," the "holy war" if we recognize these abstractions as representing Higher Authority: the parent of the dependency fantasy who protects, rewards, and punishes.

Appreciation of the power and ubiquitous nature of the dependency fantasy helps us to understand how, at every level of government and society, people set aside any doubts by assuming that "they" must know what they are doing. Often, "they" are not to be found. Even national leaders can react like small children ready to believe that the driver of the car must be wise. But the "shepherds" are not different from the "sheep."

5 Devaluing the Outsider

THE SECURITY OF A CULT is bound up with the idea of being special, better than those outside the group. Indeed, outsiders are likely to be seen as threatening because they do not share the cult's belief in the leader and in the special entitlement of its members. This threat is met by devaluing the non-believers. In part, this devaluation is an expression of the child's wish that his or her parents be the most powerful, that they know everything and can obtain for their children good things which others do not have. Furthermore, feeling blessed and favored confers a sense of protection, calming anxieties about the world outside.

Devaluing the outsider is probably the most common cult-like behavior in everyday society, where it takes the form of regarding one's opponents as if they were a homogeneous group with only negative traits. Bad motives are attributed to the other, but not to oneself. This devaluation is usually done by designating the adversary as, for example, "stupid," "rigid," "lazy," "reactionary," "bleeding heart," or "cold." When one devalues another no real proof is offered. There is seldom any inquiry into the actual statements and actions of members of the "bad" group, or any serious consideration of the adversary's point of view and its possible validity, and critical analysis of one's own "good" view, discriminating between assumptions and facts, rarely takes place.

Examples of this everyday cult behavior can be found on radio talk shows. One major program I have encountered has a host who is perpetually exclaiming at the stupidity of whatever political or bureaucratic figure is the target for the day. He and the caller-in indulge in a festival of indignation and self-congratulation, shaking their collective heads over the "ridiculous" actions that have so astonished them, seldom seeking to understand how the action under attack might be reasonable from a different point of view or even being genuinely curious about it. Instead, the host and the caller engage in cult behavior. By designating someone else as bad or stupid, they are reassured that they themselves are good, their views commendable.

DEVALUATION AND PROJECTION

Perhaps the most important thing to understand about devaluing the outsider is that it is a necessary preliminary to harming others, to doing violence. Whether the conflict is between nations or individuals, the attacker devalues the victim prior to the violent act. Sociologist Jack Katz studied street gangs and juvenile delinquents and noted the special function of cursing in propelling an attack.

> Cursing . . . is a direct and effective way of doing just what it appears to do: symbolically transforming the offending party into an ontologically lower status. . . . If the other is a shit, attacking him becomes a community service—"a form of moral garbage collection performed on behalf of all decent people. . . . Cursing at once makes the accursed repulsive and conjures up an altruistic overlay for an attack on him or her.[1]

The person you devalue becomes easier to kill. But when you look at him or her, be sure you do not see who he or she really is, for if you do, you cannot believe the person is inferior to you. A man who had been a medical corpsman in Vietnam remembers the time when he was asked to guard an old Viet Cong. His prisoner looked right into his eyes, and the corpsman looked back. Then the old man was dragged to death behind a truck.

I will never forget the man's face, and I will never forget his eyes, and I will never forget holding the rifle at his face . . . I'll never forget how old he was. There was something about the internal solidity of this human being that I will never forget. . . . Something went on that changed my life.[2]

Devaluation relies heavily on projection, "a defense mechanism, operating unconsciously, in which what is emotionally unacceptable in the self is unconsciously rejected and attributed (projected) to others."[3] Projection occurs when we attribute to others those aspects of ourselves that we wish to deny. By identifying the bad impulse or trait as being outside ourselves, we can feel more secure. Thus, projection offers protection from the anxiety of being bad and the punishment of being abandoned. In addition, by making other people bad in our own mind, we can legitimize behavior toward them that would otherwise be morally unacceptable, even to the point of sanctioning cruel and vicious actions.

I saw a vivid demonstration of projection at the conclusion of a five-day group relations conference when I joined a small group that was discussing what had been learned. Opposite me was a stocky, muscular young man with a hostile demeanor. I felt that he would physically attack me if I gave him the slightest excuse. I was afraid of him. My feelings were similar to what I had felt toward school bullies when I was growing up. Because during the conference we had dealt with projection, I tried questioning myself to see if I had any aggressive impulses toward the man whom I was afraid of. Immediately, I became aware of a desire to attack, to punch him to the ground. The violence in me was unmistakable. I looked again at the young man and could not believe the transformation that had taken place. He now appeared mild, nonthreatening, a perfectly nice person. This reversal of perception had happened in that instant of recognition of my own hostile feelings. The experience was vivid, probably because the conference had been designed to intensify projective defenses, but I am sure that similar distortions of perception take place under more normal conditions and that these perceptions can also be reversed.

The effect of projection is often a perception of the other person as being fundamentally different, a morally inferior species, undeserving of empathy. Perhaps the most common form of projection is to condemn others without noting good qualities that may lessen our sense of distance between them and us. In fact, noting an enemy's less admirable similarities to us can provoke strong feelings. Many people were distressed when Hannah Arendt's study of Adolph Eichmann, the Nazi war criminal, led her to conclude that he was not diabolical, but banal, a poor thinker, common.[4] Although the research of Stanley Milgram[5] and Philip Zimbardo[6] suggests strongly that the potential for cruelty and the carrying out of heinous orders is common to all human beings, it is difficult for us to acknowledge that we may be less unlike the Nazis than we would wish. Projection protects us all from what we fear.

The more authoritarian the human social system, the more likely a separatist world view will arise because any anger or resentment stimulated in the follower by his or her submission to the leader requires displacement onto other persons—the outsider, the infidel, the nonbeliever. Feelings of rebellion toward the leader, which are defined by the group as evil, make the cult member anxious, even ready to believe in satanic possession, an apt metaphor to describe the sensation of being invaded by unwanted feelings and images. Projection and a division of humanity into the saved and the damned are called into play with increasing intensity. As a result, the more rigid the system the more powerful is the belief in the Devil or Evil—and the more violent the feelings toward the outsider.

Because projection requires the establishment of separation, of discontinuity, of fundamental differences, the person or group onto whom the badness is projected must be a "not-me," and must, in fact, be Them. Otherwise one's condemnation would rebound onto oneself. For this reason we project most often onto other nations, other racial and religious groups, opposing political parties, and economic and social classes different from our own. Those clearly not Us. However, projection may also be used in ordinary social relationships when the need to feel superior rather than inferior arises often.

Thus, we increase our moral security by seeing others as evil, stupid, backward, or arrogant. When we do this we create and maintain cult consciousness in a fashion similar to the fanatic who perceives outsiders as damned, degenerate, and suitable for killing. When average, non-fanatic citizens devalue others they rarely murder them as a consequence, but they may well acquiesce in a political order that does.

Upon reflection you can probably identify your own focus of projection, your "not-me": Republicans, Democrats, rich, poor, black, white, Christian, Jew, Muslim, Northerner, Southerner, dove, hawk, old, young, men, women. Projection is so much a part of our thinking we seldom notice it, except when someone else does it. Again, I heard a radio talk show provide a fine example when a caller made the following comment about a political candidate: "I wouldn't vote for him; he's a Southerner. They're all prejudiced."

THE CONFIDENCE OF THE RIGHTEOUS

One of the symptoms of projection is an attitude of righteousness coloring persons' statements of their beliefs and views of others. As we have seen, through projection we reassure ourselves that we are good (as in the child's world) by pointing out that someone else is bad. The covert "I am good" is signalled by self-righteousness, which requires the devaluation of someone else.

Self-righteousness is the dominant attitude of cult members, although it may be masked by false humility and public confessions of unworthiness. Righteousness has a special vocabulary that establishes two species of human beings. Reverend Jerry Falwell put it clearly: "The war is not between fundamentalists and liberals but between those who love Jesus Christ and those who hate him."[7]

Of course, the vocabulary of righteousness is seldom as stark outside of the religious or political arenas, but may include such terms as "unscientific," "neurotic," and "infantile," as opposed to "mature," "realistic," and "rigorous." Being thus negatively labeled amounts to rejection. Understandably, we are usually very sensitive to our own group's criteria for inclusion or casting-out.

Righteousness protects against self-doubt and at the same time provides a rationale for actions that would otherwise place us in the bad category. By intensifying righteousness a person can retain the feeling of being good while performing shameful acts; cruelty is justified, may even become a duty. The breaking of Clara's ties with her child, the splitting of couples, and the alienation of Hugh from his dying brother were all supposedly done for the highest spiritual reasons, as sacrifices for the high purposes of the group.

The following example of righteousness running amok is from a speech by the late Ayatollah Khomeini, who established a theocracy in Iran:

> If one permits an infidel to continue in his role as a corrupter of the earth, his moral suffering will be all the worse. If one kills the infidel, and thus stops him from perpetrating his misdeeds, his death will be a blessing to him. For if he remains alive, he will become more and more corrupt. This is a surgical operation commanded by God the all-powerful.
>
> . . . Those who have knowledge of the suffering in the life to come realize that cutting off the hand of someone for a crime he has committed is of benefit to him. In the Beyond he will thank those who, on earth, executed the will of God.[8]

There is no cruelty like the cruelty of the righteous.

Righteousness can be seen in many one would assume were not susceptible to cult thinking—scientists, for example. Proponents of theories that challenge accepted views are sometimes vilified with a zeal that combines righteousness and arrogance. One example from the history of medicine is that of the nineteenth-century Hungarian physician, I. P. Semmelweis. Semmelweis came to the conclusion that the high incidence of puerperal fever (which killed many in childbirth) among women who delivered their babies in hospitals was due to contamination by attending physicians who, at that time, routinely went from the autopsy room to the delivery room without cleansing their hands. His theory and his recommendation that physicians wash was received with such ridicule and followed by such professional persecution that he eventually went mad.

A more current example of the effects of scientific righteousness and the arrogance it fosters is provided by the development of the atomic bomb. Although the research was initially justified by the fear that the Nazis would attain the bomb first, the work did not stop when that concern was eliminated by the Allied invasion of Europe. Only one scientist left the enterprise; the rest continued what they had begun. Recently we have begun to recognize the responsibility borne by scientists for the nuclear threat that now hangs over the world. Following a reunion at Los Alamos of many who had worked on the atomic bomb, Isador Rabi, the Nobel prize-winning physicist, was asked if he thought it likely that there would ever again be such a collection of scientists working with the same dedication and idealism. "Rabi's response was unhesitating. 'I hope not,' he said. 'We had no doubts about what we were doing.'"[9]

THE POWER OF BOUNDARIES

Religions are particularly prone to devaluing outsiders because to accord outsiders equal status is to give respectability to their different versions of God and lessen the certainty of faith. Doubt may arise.

Even if the outsider is not specifically devalued, scorned, or hated, theistic religions tend to reward followers with special status: the Jews are the chosen, good Christians are saved from Hell, true Muslims go to paradise. The non-believer, in many instances, is a damned infidel. Within religions different sects or denominations vary in the absoluteness of this judgment, but the basic attitude is often the same—else why profess that faith over some other? Because my faith is true! a devout believer may exclaim.

But it is not the search for truth that leads a person to massacre or torture, to ostracize and expel, to scorn and to hate; nor is it a search for bliss or other spiritual states. In subtle or not so subtle ways, most religions use devaluation despite their best intentions. If you think not, listen closely to the next sermon you hear.

The consequences for the outsider can be significant indeed. Because religions deal in absolutes, the devaluation of the outsider can be absolute also, justifying behavior toward the innocent and helpless which the religion's founder would have condemned and which by any humane standard is barbaric. The Crusades were often a license for the murder, rape, and devastation of "infidel" peoples, those with different religious beliefs. Within Christianity, the religious passions of Catholics and Protestants fueled the Thirty Year War that almost totally destroyed Germany in the seventeenth century. More recently, Hindus and Moslims created the nightmare of fighting in Bangladesh, featuring indiscriminate slaughter and numerous examples of gang rape all under the banner of their respective religions.

Less violent forms of devaluation are almost universal. Members of most religions can be hostile, or at best uneasy, at the prospect of their children marrying outside the faith, even outside the particular sect to which they belong. When a son or daughter of Orthodox Jewish parents marries a non-Jew the parents sometimes conduct services for the dead, psychologically burying their errant child. Until 1984, a non-Catholic who married a Catholic had to sign a promise to raise their children as Catholics if the couple were to be married by a priest.

This exclusivity is not difficult to understand. All groups exist by virtue of membership boundaries; the more lax those boundaries the weaker is group cohesion and group strength. As a consequence, group boundaries are defended vigorously. Since intermarriage poses the greatest danger to religious boundaries, it is punished in overt or subtle ways; natural family ties may be subordinated to the larger religious group. As in extreme cults, family bonds may be seen as secondary to preserving the exclusiveness of the religion, the superior status of the followers and the inferior status of those outside.

Fundamentalist religions, in particular, tend to devalue the outsider to preserve the certainty of their scriptures and their leader's connection with God. In recent years, a conservative American Christian fundamentalism has experienced a resurgence and now claims many millions of members. (Since many of these fundamentalists are also members of mainline churches, it is difficult to know exactly how large the group is, but informed estimates suggest they number well over twenty million.)[10] Over recent years this movement has established powerful radio and television broadcasting networks, made extensive use of direct mail for fundraising and recruitment, and sponsored a vast increase in fundamentalist parochial schools where authoritarian, separatist, sectarian views are taught. Many teach that only "true" Christians—those "born again"—will be saved; the rest will go to Hell. However, the Jim Bakker and Jimmy Swaggart scandals did not appreciably change the popularity of these religious movements.

As evil and an assortment of devils came to dominate the consciousness of Alex Monroe and the Life Force group, Satan and evil spirits dominate the world of many fundamentalist religious sects, whether Christian, Islamic ,or of any other denomination.

HOW THE MEDIA PORTRAYS "THEM"

Media owners, editors, and reporters, like other people, are motivated by ideals, not just money or power. Most believe (some passionately) that reporting the society's imperfections and providing the public with a diversity of views and information is their special function and responsibility, that which gives meaning to their work. (I am speaking here of societies which value a free press.) The problem is that discharging that responsibility may conflict with support for the status quo. One way in which this dilemma can be solved is by being careful to report that dissent exists while devaluing it at the same time. This can be done covertly, even unconsciously, by means of the selected image.

Most newsmagazines and newspapers maintain a file of photos of prominent people and it is easy to select one in which a politician or other celebrity looks ridiculous, sinister, or ugly. Additionally, the photo can be juxtaposed with one that flatters whomever the editor wishes to promote. If you look for this device you will see it used frequently, especially at election time. Technically, it is fair, all sides are receiving publicity.

The selected image is used most powerfully by television, which presents, after all, a series of discrete scenes while attempting to convey a reality much larger than what can be framed. What the commentator or editor selects tells a part of the story, not the whole story. The power of the selected image resides in the fact that we respond to news photos and television as if they are showing us objective facts devoid of interpretation. The image seems to validate itself. Sociologist Todd Gitlin experienced this aspect of the media as a leader of Students for a Democratic Society (SDS). Later, he analyzed the media's use of the image and found that:

> . . . news photos operate under a hidden sign marked, "this really happened, see for yourself." Of course, the choice of this moment of an event as against that, of this person rather than that, of this angle rather than any other, indeed, the selection of this photographed incident to represent a whole complex chain of events and meanings, is a highly ideological procedure. But, by appearing literally to reproduce the event as it really happened, news photos suppress their selective/interpretive/ideological function. They seek a warrant in that ever pre-given, neutral structure, which is beyond question, beyond interpretation: the "real world." [11]

Television makes optimum use of this see-for-yourself power. Consequently, in many parts of the world, the nightly news shows probably shape people's perception of events more vividly and more effectively than any other source of information. Considering this power, it is worth noting that what appears on the ABC, CBS, and NBC nightly newscasts is a selection and interpretation largely created by six people, the executive producers and anchorpersons of each of the three networks.

Words also can be used quite effectively to devalue opposition. I remember how the media in the early 1960s characterized the members of SANE (myself being one of them) who opposed the atmospheric testing of nuclear weapons. While dutifully reporting our campaign, the media tended to dismiss us as having no significance; one columnist called us "small dogs barking at an express train." Being consigned to ineffective canine status was a frustrating and depressing experience. The media preferred the image of President Kennedy, who dramatically drank a glass of milk at a convention of dairy farmers to express his disdain for charges by SANE that nuclear testing was contaminating milk products with strontium 90. Fortunately, the media were wrong. After Kennedy eventually signed a treaty banning atmospheric testing, SANE acquired respect.

Reality may be distorted simply by screening out dissenting views without the outright censorship seen in totalitarian countries; reality may be distorted by giving great prominence and validity to the established view while devaluing dissenters and making them marginal. The treatment of student dissidents in the mainstream media during the 1960s offers good examples of the use of negative adjectives and selective photos combined with the ignoring or minimizing of the issues raised. As Gitlin pointed out with regard to American politics of the 1960s, an official typically was given the voice of calm rationality; dissidents were often portrayed as unreasonable, naive, impulsive, ridiculous, violent, and extreme. Some may have been, to be sure, but those who were not were seldom given a forum.

> Most of the time the taken-for-granted code of "objectivity" and "balance" presses reporters to seek out scruffy-looking, chanting, "Viet Cong" flag-waving demonstrators and to counterpose them to reasonable-sounding, fact-brandishing authorities. . . . Hotheads carry on, the message connotes, while wiser heads, officials and reporters both, with superb self-control, watch the unenlightened ones make trouble.[12]

Writing about the same era, Daniel Hallin found a similar devaluation in the media, in which protest was equated with violence, authority with competence and order:

> Cronkite began one report on college antiwar protests by saying, "The Cambodia development set off a new round of antiwar demon-

strations on U.S. campuses, and not all of them were peaceful." The film report, not surprisingly, was about one of the ones that was not peaceful, and dealt mainly with the professionalism shown by the authorities who restored order.[13]

In contrast, when the protest occurs in a communist country, American news media are likely to handle it differently. During the June 1989 demonstrations in Tiananman Square, in China's capital, the students were presented in a sympathetic light; their point of view and statements by their representatives were carried by all the American media.

Of course, devaluation also takes place in the American media's coverage of international affairs. Consider the view of the Soviet Union that was maintained by our mainstream media during the Cold War. Princeton University professor Stephen Cohen describes:

> Much American commentary on Soviet affairs employs special political terms that are inherently biased and laden with double standards. . . . The United States has a government, security organizations and allies. The Soviet Union, however, has a regime, secret police and satellites. Our leaders are consummate politicians; theirs are wily, cunning or worse. We give the world information and seek influence; they disseminate propaganda and disinformation while seeking expansion and domination.[14]

Following Gorbachev's announcement of the policy of glasnost and his visit to the United States, a marked change took place in media coverage of the Soviet Union. For the first time that I can remember, television has shown me Russians in surroundings much like mine, enjoying themselves, voicing concerns for country, children, peace— Russians like us. According to my television set, Russia has undergone a chromatic revolution, as well. Where before it had been gray, now it is in color. The weather has also changed. Sunshine has occurred in Russian cities for the first time in forty years.

There is an implicit devaluation of others in nationalism. I consider myself to be internationally minded, free of jingoism. However, some years ago, curious to hear what other countries were saying about world events, I bought a short-wave radio. As I dialed from one foreign station to another, I was surprised to find that the United States was not the center of the world. In Brazil, South American affairs and not those of the United States were being discussed; in England, the focus was local politics. The effect was a little eerie; my own country seemed to have disappeared. I knew that nationalism was a pervasive phenomenon, but my own parochialism—revealed by my surprise—had been unrecognized.

SEEING THE ENEMY ABROAD

Devaluation of other nations seen as enemies is a pervasive problem for governments. An example from the Cold War era of our own negative stereotyping is the general surprise and consternation that occurred when the USSR launched Sputnik, the first satellite. Soviets, who were regarded as backward, primitive totalitarians, weren't supposed to be able to do this. Truman is said to have expressed his own surprise that "those Asiatics" could do something like that.[15] Similar surprise greeted the first test of a hydrogen bomb by the USSR.[16]

Misperception of the enemy (basically a devaluing of the foreigner), seeing its people as less advanced, less principled, less admirable, and more deserving of punishment and harsh treatment than ourselves, has affected international relations throughout history, contributing to conflict and to spirals of increased armaments. The arms race is not a new phenomenon, and the view that the enemy must be "dealt with firmly" has had adherents. Political scientist Robert Jervis, in discussing the way misperception takes place in international relations, cites two statesmen of the nineteenth century, whose devaluing statements mirror each other:

> [James Polk:] . . . if Congress faultered [sic] or hesitated in their course, John Bull would immediately become arrogant and more grasping in his demands; & that such had been the history of the Brittish [sic] Nation in all their contests with other Powers for the last two hundred years.[17]

[Lord Palmerston:] A quarrel with the United States is . . . undesirable . . . [but] in dealing with Vulgar minded Bullies, and such unfortunately the people of the United States are, nothing is gained by submission to Insult & wrong; on the contrary the submission to an Outrage only encourages the commission of another and a greater one—such people are always trying how far they can venture to go; and they generally pull up when they find they can go no further without encountering resistance of a formidable Character.[18]

Polk was ready to see Britain as responding only to "firmness," meaning force, while Palmerston had the same view of the United States. Each was the outsider to the other and, accordingly, was devalued to maintain the righteousness and purity of the home nation's position, as in the following (one of countless modern examples of reciprocal devaluation):

[John Foster Dulles:] Khrushchev does not need to be convinced of our good intentions. He knows we are not aggressors and do not threaten the security of the Soviet Union.[19]

[Khrushchev:] It is quite well known that if one tries to appease a bandit by first giving him one's purse, then one's coat, and so forth, he is not going to be more charitable because of this, he is not going to stop exercising his banditry. On the contrary, he will become ever more insolent.[20]

The righteous indignation of contemporary leaders echoes statespersons throughout history who have believed that the armaments of others demonstrate aggressive intentions but did not apply that reasoning to arms build-ups of their own. The psychological problem is that recognizing these internal concerns would soften the distinction between good and evil governments and suggest areas of uncomfortable similarity.

Devaluation of the enemy played a role in the Bay of Pigs disaster. Journalist Peter Wyden believes it was a pivotal factor:

The final arrogance, the failure to inform themselves about Castro's strength and his people's spirit or even to inform their own infiltration teams, I attribute to the gook syndrome. American policymakers suffer from it chronically. They tend to underestimate grossly the capabilities and determination of people who committed the sin of not having been born Americans, especially "gooks" whose skins are less than white.[21]

The same devaluation, leading to far more tragic blunders, took place later in Southeast Asia. Shad Meshad, who had been a psychology officer in Vietnam, recalls his attitude:

> I was from the southeastern part of the United States, and spent my entire life there. . . . I knew nothing about Asians. The only thing I did know about them were the names we gave them, both four-letter words, "gook" and "dink." And our attitude was that the only good dink is a dead dink. This was my introduction to the culture of Asia'[22]

Devaluing the outsider is made manifest in righteousness, in blindness to the implications of one's own behavior, in the refusal to acknowledge similar intentions on both sides, in the identification of the other as bad in contrast to oneself as good. All these are hallmarks of cult behavior. While examples of this abound on both sides of the iron curtain, Ronald Reagan provided a prime specimen in his "evil empire" speech:

> Let us be aware that while they [the Soviet Union] preach the supremacy of the state, declare its omnipotence over individual man, and predict its eventual domination of all peoples on the Earth— they are the focus of evil in the modern world. . . . I urge you to beware the temptation of pride—the temptation of blithely declaring yourselves above it all and label both sides equally at fault, to ignore the facts of history and the aggressive impulses of an evil empire, to simply call the arms race a giant misunderstanding and thereby remove yourself from the struggle between right and wrong and good and evil.[23]

Certainly when one considers Stalin's starvation of the kulaks, the monstrous gulag prison system, or the barbarities the Soviets have committed in Afghanistan, there is justification for the use of the term evil. Reagan's speech, however, showed no awareness of moral lapses of our own, which, although markedly different in degree, are not so totally different in kind as to justify the self-righteousness of his pronouncement.

Unwillingness to acknowledge one's own evil is characteristic of all government leaders. It is precisely that need for purity of self-image, for displacement of all badness onto the enemy, that is "the temptation of pride" of which Reagan spoke, but did not apply to himself. In that same speech, in complete innocence of the image's applicability to himself, he cited C. S. Lewis:

> The greatest evil is not done now in those sordid "dens of crime" that Dickens loved to paint. It is not even done in concentration camps and labor camps. In those we see its final result. But it is conceived and ordered (moved, seconded, carried, and minuted) in clean, carpeted, warmed, and well-lighted offices, by quiet men with white collars and cut fingernails and smooth-shaven cheeks who do not need to raise their voice.[24]

THE COST OF DEVALUATION

In every person's life, given a psychologically threatening situation, devaluation can extend to friends with the consequence that slights and insults may be perceived when none is intended. I remember hearing Abraham Maslow, the psychologist who helped create humanistic psychology, as he reminisced about his life and spoke of his sense that his own death was near. Shortly before, he had made a pilgrimage across the United States to visit all the people with whom he had once been friends but had fallen out. He wanted to understand what had happened. What he learned was sad, ironic, and hopeful at the same time. In each case he and the friend had had an interaction whose meaning was ambiguous; Maslow might have ignored an invitation or the other person might have behaved coldly toward him. Of all the possible explanations that he or his friend considered at the time—he's worried about his job, he forgot, he is ill, he's angry at me, he dislikes me—each placed at the top of the list the explanation that was least flattering to himself. And in every case each was wrong.

I call this the Maslow principle and frequently tell the story to my patients, since the problem comes up so often. Even in daily life, it is often difficult to realize that the other person is just like us, to see him or her at eye level. Almost everyone tends to give a negative interpretation to another person's behavior in ambiguous situations. When we do this, it seems logical; when someone else does it, we find it paranoid and hard to believe.

Governments, composed of people, behave no differently. As Jervis points out, they usually view the actions of other governments as deliberate and give scant consideration to the possibility that confusion, chaos, accidents, and coincidence may be responsible; that the consequences of the other's actions may have been unintended.

Although stupidity and confusion may be responsible for a particular government action (these factors operate at least as frequently as cunning and deceit), they are seldom given much weight when analyzing the actions of an opposing country. When the German battleship Goeben escaped from a superior British force at the beginning of World War I, the Germans tried to understand why the escape had been possible. "To attribute this coup to a blunder on the part of the British admiral in command seemed so unlikely that Bethmann-Hollweg and the German Chief of the Admiralty were inclined to conclude that Britain was unwilling to strike any 'heavy blows' against Germany."[25] The Germans ended up seriously miscalculating British intentions, with very adverse consequences for Germany.

Everyday paranoia can extend to the business world, where the battle is economic; cultural differences may be ignored in favor of explanations assuming craftiness or conspiracy. For example, discussions over the joint production of the Concorde almost broke down and aborted the project when the French preference for Cartesian precision ran up against British preference for cautious empiricism:

> Unfortunately [this preference] tends to make the French suspect the British more often of duplicity than of simplicity. . . . One British aircraft executive involved [in conversations with the French over the Concorde] was reported as having complained that: "The French

always think we're being Machiavellian, when in fact we're just muddling through." [26]

In more recent years we have had a devastating illustration of the price of devaluing the outsider—the failure of our society to respond adequately to the AIDS epidemic. Randy Shilts, in his book, *And the Band Played On,* chronicled the lost opportunities to control the disease, the needless deaths of thousands of people, and the even greater losses to come in future years as a consequence of this neglect. [27]

The reason for our failure is clear. From early on, when its effects first appeared as a high incidence of Kaposi's Sarcoma, AIDS was regarded as a disease of homosexuals. In mainstream American society, homosexuals were outsiders, ridiculed, feared, and often despised as alien. Because it was homosexuals who were dying, few people outside that group cared. Extreme fundamentalists regarded AIDS as God's punishment, and others felt it served "them" right.

In contrast, Legionnaire's Disease had evoked an instant, fully mobilized response by health agencies, the government, and the media, even though it was a less deadly, less horrible killer than AIDS. In the first twelve months of the AIDS epidemic, the Center for Disease Control had spent one million dollars compared to nine million dollars spent on Legionnaire's Disease.

Newspapers paid little notice to the growing AIDS disaster until intravenous drug users were afflicted. Drug addicts, too, are outcasts, but they are more often heterosexual. The first coverage of the epidemic by *Wall Street Journal* came in 1982 under the headline, "New, Often-Fatal Illness in Homosexuals Turns Up in Women, Heterosexual Males."

Shilts's chronology of the disease is a chilling portrayal of the effects that devaluing the outsider can have upon the outcast group and, eventually, upon those who cast them out as well. After four years, AIDS cases in the United States totaled 9,000 and of these 4,300 people had died. No massive response by the government or the media had yet taken place.

To appreciate the magnitude of these figures it should be recalled that Legionnaires' disease had claimed twenty-nine lives, the poisoned Tylenol capsules had caused seven deaths. Both of these crises elicited mobilization of all the resources the nation could muster and front-page, extensive coverage by the news media.

Not until the middle of the 1980s, when it became clear that AIDS could strike anyone, did the media give AIDS the full treatment and the government followed suit. Unfortunately, by then there were 12,000 cases, 6,000 people had died, and a virus whose latency can run eight years or more was lodged in tens of thousands who would yet fall ill. As of February 1990, reported AIDS cases totaled 121,000, with 72,000 deaths. In 2002, the worldwide death toll is estimated to reach tens of millions.

Shilts describes how in Washington Arthur Bennet, an AIDS sufferer, stood in the rain with other protesters and gestured toward the White House, saying, "I think in the beginning of this whole syndrome, that they, over there, and a lot of other people said, 'Let the faggots die. They're expendable.' I wonder if it would have been 1,500 Boy Scouts, what would have been done." [28]

6 Avoiding Dissent

ALTHOUGH WE ALL NEED DISSENT as a corrective, cults tend to punish it, to inhibit and stifle disagreement and criticism, to restrict access to information that would challenge group beliefs.

Cults employ a variety of means to exclude dissent. Mail may be monitored or withheld, only certain literature allowed, and discordant views may be labeled bad or satanic. In addition, members' attention is confined to a narrow field; if free time is spent studying and reciting dogma there is less danger that subversive information will be encountered or, if it is, that it will be thought about and its implications understood. Dogma itself may be simplified into slogans, rendering members' thinking even more primitive and further hampering critical thought. These means are enhanced by the punishment the group and leader mete out for challenging authority.

Such coercive forces create conflicts. The cult member wishes to continue riding in the back seat of the car, but at the same time his or her self-respect is threatened by compliance with censorship and subjection to rewards and punishments. So the inhibition of dissent may be pushed out of awareness, become unconscious. Conscious and unconscious suppression and restriction of dissent is perhaps the most characteristic feature of cult life; the more severe the restriction, the more control exercised by the group and the leader.

Cults further restrict dissent through decreased contact with non-members. Outsiders are likely to raise critical questions about the leader and the group's activities, thus weakening the group fantasy. In addition, as discussed earlier, outsiders are a threat because they may be sources of support, self-esteem, and comfort, offsetting the need for the group. Research suggests that the fewer social ties a cult convert had before joining, the more likely it was that he or she would remain in the organization.[1] When Hugh and Clara Robinson finally made their escape from Life Force, their contact with outsiders was crucial.

UNSPOKEN BOUNDARIES IN THE MEDIA

Avoidance of dissent is a prominent feature of normal society. We assume that in the United States our free press (including radio and television) voices all the dissent we would need. There is no government censorship; the First Amendment shields the media from interference. However, although America's mainstream media pride themselves on being independent, balanced, objective, in practice those characteristics are more limited than most, including media personnel, realize. Dissent is exercised within certain unspoken boundaries; beyond those limits it is avoided, downplayed, or ignored. Because the mass media are the major source of many kinds of information for the public at large, media behavior has far-reaching effects. The media can create by what it presents.

Ben Bagdikian, dean of the Graduate School of Journalism at the University of California, Berkeley (and former reporter, journalist, and *Washington Post* editor), comments on two key findings of his research on the mass media:

> What the public learns is heavily weighted by what serves the economic and political interests of the corporations that own the media . . .
>
> The naivete of working journalists about the influence of owners on the news they publish is more widespread than even my thirty years as a reporter and editor had led me to believe.[2]

Although our media enjoy great freedom, they are in a dependent relationship to three types of authority: the corporate world that owns them, the advertisers that provide their revenues, and the government figures upon whom they rely for information. These dependency relationships involve both conscious and unconscious pressures that result in an inhibition of dissent not usually noticed by the public or by reporters and journalists themselves.

SELECTIVE REPORTING

Six large corporations own almost all of the 25,000 principal media outlets. The boards of directors controlling the corporations are composed of people who also serve on the boards of other corporations, many of them advertisers, forming an interlocking network. This concentration of media power in the hands of a relatively few big businesses and financial institutions makes it possible for these organizations to exert behind-the-scenes control over our access to information.[3]

Bagdikian's work offers suggestive instances of corporate control. One case involved the Tribune Company of Chicago, publishers of the *Chicago Tribune*. A member of its board of directors was also a director of Sears, Roebuck at the time the Federal Trade Commission accused Sears of dishonest sales promotion and advertising. The *Chicago Tribune* did not report this news at all even the though Sears national headquarters is in Chicago and the accusation would undoubtedly have been of interest to its readers.[4]

The *San Francisco Chronicle* noted a more recent example:

A reference to the General Electric Co., which owns NBC, was removed from a report on shoddy products that was televised Thursday by the network's "Today" program.

The report focused on a federal investigation of inferior bolts used by U.S. industries in products such as airline jets and missile silos.

It included a reference to a discovery by engineers at General Electric that one of every three bolts used in their jet engines is inferior.[5]

Bagdikian cites other instances of what appear to be outright censorship—books that aroused corporate displeasure being pulled before, during, or after publication. These include *Counter-Revolutionary Violence* by Noam Chomsky, *Dupont: Behind the Nylon Curtain* by Gerard Zilg, *Countercoup: The Struggle for the Control of Iran* by Kermit Roosevelt, and *Corporate Murder* by Mark Dowie.[6]

Clearly books are published and documentaries aired that are critical of the corporate world; newspapers and newsmagazines publish exposes of business or government leaders. However, the potential for control exists and may be exercised in more subtle ways than cancelling a book. Certain ideas that serve advertisers and business may be cultivated and established as fact in the minds of the general public. One example is the general belief that unions have caused a drop in American productivity, whereas from 1981 to 1987, the productivity of U.S. manufacturing workers as a whole increased an average of 4 percent, while hourly wages increased only 0.8 percent.[7] Unions undoubtedly have their own illusions, but it is the corporate view that tends to be voiced in the media serving the majority of our citizens.

Nicholas Johnson, formerly a Federal Communications Commission department head for eleven years, put the problem most directly: "The First Amendment rights belong to the owners, and the owners can exercise those rights by hiring people who will hire journalists who don't rock the boat, who don't attack advertisers, who don't challenge the establishment."[8]

ADVERTISING'S COVERT INDOCTRINATION

The mass media also do little to inform their audiences of the power of advertisers to control the ideological content of media entertainment—and, on occasion, media commentary. As the major revenue source for television, radio, and newspapers, advertisers have considerable influence over what appears. Their financial leverage is huge; back in 1981, media businesses earned thirty-three billion dollars from advertisers compared to seven billion dollars from readers and viewers.[9] Today, the money involved is much greater; the one who pays the piper often calls the tune. The American public sees itself at least somewhat through the special vision of advertisers.

Effects of advertiser influence were suggested by research at the Annenberg School of Communication that showed the world portrayed by television to be quite unrealistic.

> Despite the fact that nearly half of the national income goes to the top fifth of the real population, the myth of [the] middle class as the all-American norm dominates the world of television. . . . Blue-collar and service work occupies 67 percent of all Americans but only 10 percent of television characters. . . . [On television] men outnumber women at least three to one . . . older people (over 65) [comprise] one-fifth of their true proportion in the population . . .[10]

The prime American consumer is between eighteen and forty-nine years of age, white, upwardly mobile, and middle- or upper-middle-class and this is the group advertisers are most interested in reaching. The effect on the media audience is significant; viewers of low socioeconomic status who watch television four or more hours per day are more likely to call themselves middle-class than their light-viewing (less than two hours daily) counterparts.

Overall, the Annenberg researchers found that television exerts a homogenizing effect.

> Viewing blurs traditional differences, blends them into a more homogeneous mainstream, and bends the mainstream toward a "hard line" position on issues dealing with minorities and personal rights. Hard-nosed commercial populism, with its mix of restrictive conservatism and pork-chop liberalism, is the paradoxical—and potentially volatile—contribution of television to political orientations.[11]

This shaping of reality is not a matter of chance. Some years ago, at FCC hearings in 1965 to determine how much influence advertisers had on non-commercial content of television and radio, representatives of

Procter & Gamble testified to a set of quite explicit rules for television programs in which they would advertise.

> There will be no material on any of our programs that could in any way further the concept of business as cold, ruthless, and lacking all sentiment or spiritual motivation.
>
> If a businessman is cast in the role of villain, it must be made clear that he is not typical but is as much despised by his fellow businessmen as he is by other members of society.[12]

This is not extraordinary; if I were a major advertiser on television, I know how I would like psychiatrists to be portrayed. However, obeying the Procter & Gamble guidelines required a distortion of reality, especially as the company's instructions went beyond issues of the businessperson's image. "Where it seems fitting, the characters in Procter & Gamble's dramas should reflect recognition and acceptance of the world situation in their thoughts and actions, although in dealing with war, our writers should minimize the 'horror' aspects."[13] These instructions further specified that "some basic conception of the American way of life" must not be attacked by a character in a drama or documentary unless a rejoinder is "completely and convincingly made someplace in the same broadcast." Finally, television executives were instructed, "If there is any question whatever about such material, it should be deleted." P&G was protecting not just the business world, but also the general status quo.

That was almost thirty-five years ago, but the situation may not be different today as the media, especially newspapers, have become more and more dependent on advertiser revenues. Advertisers do not hesitate to threaten withdrawal of ads. In the case of major advertisers, such as the tobacco industry, the threat appears to be quite potent. Edith Whelan, a journalist with the American Council on Science and Health, reported in 1980 that she had approached the leading women's magazines (*Cosmopolitan, Harper's Bazaar, Ladies Home Journal, Mademoiselle, Ms., McCall's, Redbook, Seventeen, Vogue,* and *Working Woman*) asking them to run articles on the growing incidence of smoking-induced disease in women. All these magazines had run articles supporting the Equal Rights Amendment, but in this case they refused. Whelan commented, "I frequently wrote on health topics for women's magazines, and have been told repeatedly by editors to stay away from the subject of tobacco." [14]

As another example, Bagdikian reports that in 1981 a senior vice president of MGM told newspaper executives that there had been too many negative film reviews and that they could not take for granted the five hundred million dollars in ads that the industry place with them. Sounding much like Procter & Gamble he warned, "Today the daily newspaper does not always create a climate that is supportive and favorable to the motion picture industry . . . gratuitous and hateful reviews threaten to cause the romance between newspapers and the motion picture industry to wither on the vine." [15]

Control of content is not exerted by advertising interests alone, but also by the owners of the media who hire and fire media personnel. Under normal circumstances media personnel have considerable latitude in what they present, but according to Bagdikian's research that latitude has its limits; what is not allowed is criticism of the free enterprise system itself. Writing in 1987, he commented:

> Some reporters often criticize specific corporate acts, to the rage of corporate leaders. But the taboo against criticism of the system of contemporary enterprise is, in its unspoken way, almost as complete within mainstream journalism and broadcast programming in the United States as criticism of communism is explicitly forbidden in the Soviet Union. [16]

Bagdikian predicts that if the time came when corporations felt they were in fundamental jeopardy, nothing would prevent them from exercising their power of ownership to protect their interests.

Particularly in television, advertisers and the corporate world have been very influential in defining us to ourselves. The materialism and superficiality of most television programs, and the emphasis on a world of middle-class whites between eighteen and forty-nine, is not necessarily what the public wants, as television executives claim, but what the advertisers demand. Such covert indoctrination is typical of cults.

In this instance it is not a particular religion or philosophy being served, but rather the enhancement of desire, the selling of products, the protection of the status quo. The effects of this indoctrination are a measure of the power of the media—and those who influence it—to shape our perception, to establish the climate of belief in which we live.

OFFICIALLY SANCTIONED TRUTHS

Although they regard themselves as watchdogs in an adversarial role, media people are dependent on governmental authority because they rely heavily on access to the White House, Congress, and cabinet officials and on maintaining special relationships with contacts at the Pentagon, the Food and Drug Administration, or whatever government agencies are relevant to their assignments. The authorities can reward favored journalists with inside information and news scoops or penalize them by denying access. Bernard Roshco described a type of incident that occurs frequently enough to remind reporters that cooperation is essential to their livelihood. At a 1969 Nixon press conference, Stuart Loory, then the *Los Angeles Times'* White House correspondent questioned the president:

> In response to the President's statement that he favored neither instant segregation nor instant integration, Loory asked whether the years 1954 through 1968 could be termed "instant." The result was that Loory began losing his access to the news. He was dumped from the Air Force One press pool. On one Nixon trip to California, when the President invited several reporters to interview him while walking on the beach, Loory was left out even though his was the home paper and would have devoted much more space to the event. And *Los Angeles Times* reporters were not invited to Administration background briefings held to discuss the next year's State of the Union message.[17]

Consciously or unconsciously, every reporter must decide whether or not he or she wants to be another Stuart Loory. Without allowing themselves to notice, reporters may adjust their views or engage in internal censorship to minimize conflict with authority. Thus, their self-image of independence and objectivity can be preserved, and their access to the "source." Their suppression of dissent becomes unconscious.

All reporters assigned to a particular beat (for example, the Pentagon or the State Department) are subject to these influences. They need access to their sources, who in turn have their own needs for media attention. This mutual obligation system is likely to co-opt the reporter who, over time, becomes part of the institution he is covering. Warren Weaver, of the *New York Times*, pointed to this problem in his book *Both Your Houses*:

> Institutional reporting has its advantages—members are more cooperative with reporters whom they come to sense as acolytes of the establishment—but the pitfalls are deep and dangerous. A reporter who has been admitted into the inner circle, or even allowed to peep in occasionally from the edge, is likely to be protective of the man who admitted him and of those observed there.[18]

A reporter may begin to identify with the source's point of view, to adopt a posture that is harmonious with the aims of the people he or she needs. News coverage is necessarily selective and the selection process may work unconsciously to omit items that would spoil a reporter's relationship with the source and to focus on those that will enhance it.

Mark Hertsgaard, a journalist who investigated the relationship between the press and the Reagan presidency, found a similar problem:

> Indeed, the political effect of most news coverage was to fill people's heads with officially sanctioned truth. . . . This was to be expected; after all, the press took its definition of what constituted political news from the political governing class in Washington. Thus while the press shaped mass opinion, it reflected elite opinion; indeed, it effectively functioned as a mechanism by which the latter was transformed, albeit imperfectly, into the former.[19]

This unconscious process of accommodation and compliance is similar in kind to that which Hugh and Clara Robinson experienced in

Life Force. Their dependence on Alex Monroe for advancement, favors, and continued status led them to support policies and behavior that they might otherwise have challenged. Their support of Alex was rationalized, using the group's dogma; critical thoughts were pushed aside.

SELF-CENSORSHIP IN THE MEDIA

On the one hand, media workers are interested in attracting the public interest by reporting dramatic conflicts in the social, economic, and political system of which they are a part. On the other hand, they are also interested in sustaining the system that produces the revenues that pay their salaries. The owners of the media feel comfortable with the establishment of which they are privileged members and in which they believe.

Media bias in favor of the status quo is often not obvious because of the appearance of debate in the various mass media presentations, especially network television. However, debate turns out to be within the rather narrow limits acceptable to authority. Some years ago, a study was conducted of the guest list of ABC's "Nightline." The analysis covered a forty-month period (1 January 1985 to 30 April 1988). Not counting ABC staff members, five guests appeared more than ten times: Henry Kissinger (fourteen), Alexander Haig (fourteen), Eliot Abrams (twelve), Reverend Jerry Falwell (twelve), Alejandro Bendana of Nicaragua's Foreign Office (eleven).

According to the study, this distribution is characteristic. Conservative and right-wing spokespersons, and government and ex-government officials dominated the airtime. Left-wing, "radical" spokespersons were usually from foreign countries. (Counting only American guests who appeared more than five times, there were nineteen, all men. The woman who appeared most frequently was Jean Kirkpatrick. All guests were white except for Jesse Jackson and Harry Edwards. Of the nineteen who appeared frequently, thirteen were conservative, most connected in some way to the Reagan administration. Labor, public interest, and social or ethnic leaders accounted for only 5.7 percent of the U.S. guest list.)[20]

Such bias can be quite invisible to the editors and producers themselves. Their pride and belief in their independence reflects the fact that they are rarely subject to crude arm twisting as to what or what not to present to the public. But their dependence on media owners and the government elite for financial rewards, information, and position can exert an insidious form of control—as it does in cults. The whole process can take place automatically, smoothly, even for those with more time for considered decisions than the average gatekeeper. Fred Freed, a producer of outstanding NBC public affairs programs reflected, "I have never been turned down for a program I wanted to do for censorship reasons. On the other hand I'm not sure I have ever asked to do one I knew management would not approve for these reasons."[21]

The result of media self-censorship is a tendency toward perpetuation of the assumptions fundamental to the government and business interests on which the media depend. This can have particularly far-reaching consequences in foreign affairs. During the early years of the Vietnam War most within the media did not question Cold War ideology, but continued to present the government's picture of a world divided into two camps, the free world and the communist, the latter assumed to be directed by Moscow through proxy armies in China, Cambodia, Vietnam, and elsewhere. This simplistic, ahistorical view supported the domino theory and justified intervention all over the world as vital to United States interests. Political scientist Daniel Hallin, who studied the role of the media during the Vietnam War, found that television coverage did not often directly confront administration premises. Commentators and journalists disputed the effectiveness of government policies, but, all in all:

> . . . none of the larger questions posed by the war was raised in any substantial way in the news. There was no discussion of the origins of revolution. . . . There was no second look at the doctrine of containment or its application to a conflict like Vietnam.[22]

Late in the war, when pressure for withdrawal began to mount, the media shifted to a more oppositional stance, but still within certain limits:

Vietnam fits a pattern that has often been observed in situations of political crisis: the media in such periods typically distance themselves from incumbent officials and their policies, moving in the direction of an "adversary" conception of their role. But they do not make the "system"—or its core beliefs—an issue, and if these are questioned, usually rise to their defense [emphasis added].[23]

A similar situation prevailed in most coverage of the Iran hostage crisis during the Carter administration. Sociologist David Altheide found that "the Iranian situation was reduced to one story—the freeing of the hostages—rather than coverage of its background and context, of the complexities of Iran, of alternative American policies, and of contemporary parochial politics in a world dominated by superpowers."[24]

Daniel Hallin concludes that "this is one of the most important consequences of the close connection between the modern media and government: the range of political discussion in the press is usually restricted to the policy alternatives being debated in Washington." This is true of the current response to the terrorist threat.[25]

Economist Edward Herman and Noam Chomsky, philosopher and linguist, did extensive research on media coverage of Latin America and Indochina. They found a consistent pattern of "worthy and unworthy" victims. As an example, they contrasted the news coverage of the murder of a Polish priest, Jerszy Popieluszko, killed by the Polish police in October 1984, with the coverage of the murders of a large number of Latin American religious figures in El Salvador and Guatemala. The victims of communist governments received extensive coverage—they were apparently worthy. The victims of governments supported by the U.S. received scanty treatment, qualitatively different as well as much reduced in scope—they were apparently unworthy. The worthy received dramatic treatment and demands for justice; the unworthy mostly low-key, sparse descriptions accompanied by regrets about the violence from both left and right. The notion that the governments of Guatemala and El Salvador are reformist and centrist has been the official position of the Carter, Reagan, and Bush administrations, despite abundant evidence to the contrary. Herman and Chomsky make a compelling case for consistent media bias expressed with few exceptions through selective emphasis and by ignoring or downplaying contradictory testimony. The authors suggest that an additional factor may bias reporting on Latin America:

> Western reporters are very rarely physically threatened—let alone murdered—in Poland, the Soviet Union, Cuba, or Nicaragua. They are often threatened and sometimes murdered in El Salvador, Guatemala, and other U.S. clients in Latin America. This irony is not commented upon in the free press, nor are the effects of this potential and actual violence against dissident reporters on the possibilities of honest reporting.[26]

Thus, there is much evidence that the mainstream mass media, controlled by corporate and financial interests, dominated by advertisers, and dependent on government sources generally reflect the point of view and interests of these groups. (There are notable exceptions, such as the CBS documentaries: *Hunger* and *The Selling of the Pentagon*, but covert conformity is the rule; in fact, these documentaries resulted in the network being investigated by the government agencies that they criticized.) As media commentator Herbert Gans observes, it is rare to read or see in the mainstream media any discussion of why wealth is distributed so unequally in our country and between the developing and developed nations, or of the power of corporations over the average citizen.[27]

How shall we understand the media's support of the status quo? Are the mass media just propaganda machines, as Herman and Chomsky suggest? These authors show bias that exists, but they write as if media complicity is conscious. In some cases it may be, but I suggest that to a significant degree the processes that lead to bias operate outside awareness, as in cults; the politically correct and the economically expedient are internalized, become unconscious, and are reinforced by the group, which includes the public.

The assumptions that constitute the status quo are recycled for corporate owners, for advertisers, for government officials, as well as for the public. The limits defined by authorities are accepted unnoticed by almost everyone. Bagdikian concludes that "the butcher's thumb that quietly tilts news in favor of corporate values has survived the rise in journalistic standards. The tilt has been so quietly and steadily integrated into the normal process of weighing news that the angle of the needle is now seen as 'zero'." [28]

WANTING TO BELIEVE DOESN'T MAKE IT SO

Within the corporate world, the more authoritarian the leadership structure, the less dissent is appreciated, and the more emphasis is given to loyalty to prevailing corporate views. Former General Motors executive John De Lorean describes how this loyalty was manifested:

> If your appearance, style and personality were consistent with the corporate stereotype, you were well on your way to being a "loyal" employee. But loyalty demanded more. It often demanded personal fealty, actual subservience to the boss . . .
>
> Lower executives, eager to please the boss and rise up the corporate ladder, worked hard to learn what he wanted or how he thought on a particular subject. They then either fed the boss exactly what he wanted to know, or they modified their own proposals to suit his preferences. [29]

The devaluation and suppression of dissent can lead to financially disastrous corporate decisions or to violations of moral principles. The history of the Corvair is a case in point. As originally designed, the car had a tendency to flip over when making turns at high speed. According to John De Lorean, the problem was well known to the GM engineers, a number of whom fought to modify the car's suspension or keep it out of production. They were overruled by the general manager and finally told to stop objecting and "get on the team." The Corvair was produced and sold. De Lorean commented, "I don't think any one car before or since produced as gruesome a record on the highway as the Corvair." [30]

The costliest failure in the history of magazine publishing occurred when top executives of Time, Inc. pushed ahead with a project to publish a weekly broadcast and cable television listings magazine, *Television-Cable Week,* without the market testing recommended by their own researchers and without first solving major problems which other subordinates had brought to management's attention. A former member of the editorial management team described how adverse facts were shunted aside and deleted from the final presentation to the board of directors: "Sutton listened earnestly as Grum continued with his advice: keep the presentation simple, emphasize the up-side, and above all do not dwell on the complexities and uncertainties—the very risks that the task force had highlighted in the January presentation."[31]

Time, Inc. proceeded to lose forty-five million dollars on a magazine that ran for only six months. Not only did the board members uncritically accept the optimistic presentation, so did a Wall Street brokerage firm.

> Munro and his associates were preaching to an audience that was eager to believe. One of the analysts at the gathering, Alan Gottesman, summed up his reaction to the presentation this way: "Hell, if you hear the company's top men say they've got some new breakthrough computer system to publish the magazine, you're going to believe them, right?"[32]

Wanting to believe is perhaps the most powerful dynamic initiating and sustaining cult-like behavior. Hugh and Clara Robinson accepted Alex Monroe's rationalizations for behavior that they would otherwise have labeled immoral, selfish, or cruel. Along with fear, the need to believe caused them to rationalize their own behavior and continue in Life Force long after the evidence of degeneration was in plain view to the outsider. A similar process seems responsible for the Corvair and *Television-Cable Week* fiascos. Dissenting voices that could have brought more reality to the decision-making process were ignored or suppressed. Wanting to believe affects everyone, leaders and followers alike.

The avoidance of dissent is almost automatic where unequal power exists and the leader makes it clear that being contradicted is displeasing, even dangerous. Dissent can only be used if the leader and the group value it, understand its necessity and demonstrate that dissent is welcome. In the corporate world, dissent is avoided and suppressed the more a CEO is unwilling to occupy an eye-level world with subordinates and insists on their gazing upward at him or her.

The leader is not the only inhibiting force, the group as a whole can make its displeasure known if dissent focuses on areas of group vulnerability such as immoral corporate behavior, over-optimism, leadership mistakes, and paranoia. Even if a corporate CEO welcomes dissent, lower-level executives may stifle contrary opinion so that it never reaches him or her. Something like this appears to have been responsible for the space shuttle Challenger disaster. As described by Henry Cooper, Jr. in the *New Yorker,* Thiokol engineers voiced their concerns about the safety of the O-ring seal and believed the launch should be canceled, particularly as the air temperature at the launch site was lower than for any previous test measurements. Overruled by company officials, their objections were not passed on to those with final authority for the launch.[33]

Lower-level censorship is particularly likely when leadership wants condensed, simplified reports and summaries on which to base decisions. Unpleasant facts and possibilities are easier to prune and may be given shorter shrift than optimistic, forward-looking statements.

Avoidance of dissent is often confused with loyalty. Authoritarian leaders tend to regard loyalty as the foremost virtue of subordinates. Peter Wyden described how at the final meeting before the invasion of Cuba, Rusk, Nitze, and Bundy all set aside doubts and questions in order to "close ranks with the president" and vote in favor of the invasion.[34]

Only a lively appreciation of dissent's vital function at all levels of society can preserve it as a corrective to wishful thinking, self-inflation, and unperceived rigidity.

WHO GETS TO CHOOSE?

The word heretic is derived from the Greek *hairetikos*, meaning "able to choose." All too frequently, administrators of religions consider themselves to be God's representatives and define any choice of doctrine or interpretation but theirs as false or evil. To the extent that religious leaders claim divine authority, dissent is discouraged and suppressed among their followers. Although differences of interpretation of holy writ always arise, when these differences are substantial they may not be tolerated. If dissenters are expelled or leave, a new religion may result; many different sects have arisen in all the major religions. When an individual defies doctrinal authority—becomes a heretic—and the difference in interpretation is deemed dangerous to the faith of true believers, punishment may be severe, barbaric. Muslim clergy tortured and killed Hallaj, the Sufi saint, for saying, "I am God." Clergy of the Inquisition tortured and burned Christians who were far less challenging but were suspected of having the wrong beliefs.

Some choices are not permitted and dissent is punished, even in today's modern, pluralistic western world. A recent example is Pope John Paul II's attempt to banish dissent by revoking the right of a distinguished Catholic scholar, the Reverend Charles Curran, to teach at Catholic University. Curran had dissented at some points from non-infallible but traditional church teachings on sexual ethics. Archbishop Hickey explained the unusual and severe step taken by the Pope: ". . . the Holy See has gone on to clarify for us, to say there is no right to public dissent . . ."[35] A Vatican official commented further that "we now have a situation in the United States where many theologians teach not only church doctrine but also the dissident view. . . . Then these professors ask the students to pick their choice . . . an absolutely unacceptable practice."[36]

Whatever one's position on dissent in the theological domain, it is clear that such an authoritarian attitude is incompatible with democratic government. Fundamentalist Reverend Jerry Falwell seems to agree, but finds the problem to be democracy itself:

> Today we find that America is more of a democracy than a republic. Sometimes there is mob rule. In some instances, a vocal minority prevails. Our Founding Fathers would not accept the tyranny of a democracy because they recognized that the only sovereign over men and nations was Almighty God.[37]

REINFORCING BELIEF

Members of almost all groups committed to a particular belief—be it religious or otherwise—are inclined to read and study works that confirm that belief. The dissenting views of outsiders are ignored or dismissed.

Where a religious group's security and the leader's power is heavily committed to infallibility, the extra precaution of direct censorship, including the burning of books, is taken, as occurred most recently in Iran. For centuries the Catholic Church maintained an Index of condemned books Catholics could not read without special permission because their faith or morals might be disturbed. Recently, Christian fundamentalists have tried to remove from American classrooms such diverse works as *Of Mice and Men, A Farewell to Arms, The Grapes of Wrath, 1984, Catch 22,* and even *The American Heritage Dictionary.*[38] There has been an ongoing battle to curtail the teaching of evolution and great concern with the evils of "secular humanism."

To read or to listen to differing or opposing views is to court disturbance, trouble, doubt. Billy Graham puts it thus: "The world longs for authority, finality, and conclusiveness. It is weary of theological floundering and uncertainty. Belief exhilarates the human spirit; doubt depresses."[39]

The exclusion of doubt has a price. Intellectual parochialism may be fostered by restricting contact with outsiders and by building walls of indifference or, in the most extreme cases, hate.

When religions provide schooling for members' children, such schools may isolate the children from other worldviews and facilitate a portrayal of the outsider as evil or inferior. When this educational insulation is perpetuated into adulthood, cult-like abuses may arise. Until recently, the Catholic parochial school system provided recruits for seminaries and convents, which, in turn, provided teachers to perpetuate the school system. Although not all parochial schools are repressive, many have created an atmosphere of fear, guilt, and conformity. As one former nun put it, "You are taught that what is bad in you is yours; what is good in you is God's."[40] The deadening effect of such an education is attested to by ex-nuns' autobiographical accounts:

> I have been becoming more and more aware of the deadness I see all around me—the deadness of tired, tense bodies clinging to a ritual, of people who patch up life's cracks so nothing new can sink in. I see their intensity and I see their seriousness; I see their compulsive concern for the slightest deviation from the Holy Rule. And what is most frightening, I see the hugeness and monstrosity of their commitment to suffering.[41]

Christianity is not alone in providing systems that shield members from outside views. The Lubavitcher Hasidic community in Brooklyn is a case in point. Veneration of its leader approaches worship. The exclusiveness and separation of members from the larger community, enforced by unusual dress, elaborate rules and rituals, and specialized studies and language, can result in an extremely narrow and parochial outlook that is, in essence, cult-like. In a long, mostly favorable article on the Hasidic community, Liz Harris writes of being surprised when her host declared that he did not believe Jacobo Timerman's description of his incarceration and torture by Argentina authorities. Indeed, he declared there was no anti-Semitism in Argentina. The reason for his view was that Timerman was believed to be "sympathetic to the Communists." Becuase the communists were a godless people who persecuted Jews and Argentina at the time of the interview was certainly anti-communist, Timerman was not to be believed. Harris comments:

> I found it astonishing that one obvious reality, the suffering of Russian Jews, could utterly annihilate another, the suffering of Jacobo Timerman and many like him. Did it matter to Moshe that Timerman had emphatically denied any Communist sympathies? Or that fuzzy political accusations had brought about the disappearance of thousands of innocent people? The bright light that the Hasidim trained on their communal and inner life seemed to dim considerably when it was turned on the outside world—a circumstance that appeared to strain the quality of mercy hereabouts.[42]

Of course, the more a religion allows debate, discussion, and dis-agreement, the more adaptable and realistic it can be, the less captured by its form. However, this tolerance may threaten certainty, and cer-tainty (as Reverend Billy Graham testified) is one of the great attrac-tions of religious belief.

THE POWER OF SECRECY

Irving Janis, a psychologist who studied presidential advisory groups, notes that in Washington, D.C., as elsewhere, the suppression of deviant points of view is often done by subordinates to protect the president from discordant opinions that might damage their confidence. The underlying wish is to preserve for all the fantasy of the Leader.

Unless a leader clearly intends that subordinates should challenge and criticize, his or her views will meet little serious opposition. Hugh and Clara Robinson's story shows how cult followers, even without specific instructions, act to protect the position and views of their leader. In the capacity of protectors, group members may feel justified in employing threats, subterfuge, and deceit.

In our government, as in most, a principal means of avoiding dis-sent and criticism is through the use of secrecy. Nowhere has this been more manifest than in the planning of covert operations such as the overthrow of Chilean President Salvador Allende during the Nixon administration and later, the sale of arms to Iran during the Reagan administration.

Secrecy supports cult-like behavior, as we saw in the Life Force group, where the hierarchy was maintained through limiting access to infor-mation. Secrecy functions not only to cover up unethical activities from outside eyes, but also to increase authoritarian control over the larger group. By promoting the idea that the leader or the in-group have spe-cial information and expertise, they remove themselves from criticism and justify the exclusion of others from the decision-making process.

In the case of religious cults the special information and expertise is described as divine inspiration or enlightenment. The cult leader's presumed higher state precludes lower beings from judging his or her actions.[43] Similar claims are made in government where special knowledge of the enemy or secret technical information is said to justify decisions that would otherwise be objected to on moral or even practical grounds.

Secrecy is invoked often in the name of national security. Tom Wicker, a *New York Times* columnist, comments on the connotations of that term, meanings we can understand in terms of cult psychology:

> But those two words [national security] are magic, an incantation, vibrating with the ideas of power, knowledge, authority, responsibility. National security!—the phrase rings with masculinity, patriotism, heroism. Used in tones of proper solemnity by someone from the White House or the Pentagon, those words can mesmerize most Americans; and a generation of Washington reporters stood mostly in awe of them—not least, I believe, because a reporter who knows something that can't be printed for national-security reasons is elevated himself into that prized masculine circle of power, knowledge, authority, responsibility. He becomes the ultimate insider; and the reporter's deadliest enemy—the desire to be an accepted part of the world of power around him—has won its final victory.[44]

THE BENEFITS OF BEING CONTRADICTED

As Americans, we affirm the right to dissent, consider it of supreme value, make the infringement of dissent unlawful, and recognize it as basic to our political system. However, in actual practice few of us are pleased when someone disagrees with us; at best we tolerate it, inwardly we reject it. Although in our society the right to dissent is constantly affirmed, there is little indication that as individuals or in groups we value opposing views directed at ourselves. In science, within clear professional limits, there may be more appreciation of dissent, more readiness to welcome the opponent, but in general, although we may defend the right of an opponent to speak out against us we are not grateful when he or she has done so. In almost all cases we react to dissent as to an enemy, countering with argument or a patronizing dismissal. This seems natural, just "human nature." Yet considering how much of our thinking is prejudiced, rigid, and self-protective and how much we make use of inadequate and selective information, dissent deserves to be treated not as an adversary but as an ally, something that can rescue us from selective blindness, make us more realistic and thus more effective. Objectively, we should regard dissent with gratitude. It is a matter of some chagrin to me that even in the process of writing this book I find it very difficult to practice what I preach; whenever my own opinions are challenged my first response is to put up my mental fists and fight back, defending my position. Only then do I catch myself and ask the dissenter, Why do you think that?

Look around at all levels of society. The adversarial approach is ingrained; authors, radio and television commentators, spokespersons for various causes, politicians of every hue, all insist on the rightness of their own views while denigrating the opposition's. Yet life is complex; our perception and information are limited. Indeed, to some degree, everyone is in error.

Just like the members of Life Force, we want agreement for our beliefs so we can feel the security of being right. Dissent threatens that; it reduces our status, our certainty, our claim to privilege. As I remarked earlier, the problem with Reagan's "evil empire" speech was not so much that he was harshly critical of the Soviet government—surely it deserved harsh criticism—but that he did not acknowledge that we as a nation are not free from evil, even if our system is more humane.

In all the deservedly adverse comment that Reagan received for that speech, there was no recognition that similar speeches take place every day in the utterances and opinions of almost all citizens, liberal and conservative alike. Many people regarded Reagan and his conservative allies as the source of evil in this country, oblivious to the irony that in doing so they were engaging in similar thinking. Again, the key issue is not that criticism is undeserved, but that the persons dishing out criticism reserve none for themselves, nor do they acknowledge any validity to the other's position. They are not being artful. They simply cannot accept the fact that their adversary has the same self-righteous feeling as they do because the implications are uncomfortable: our own feelings of sincerity and righteousness do not certify that we are right. To welcome dissent is to accept that fact.

In ordinary life, dissent is restricted primarily by a selective focus on the familiar and the comfortable. At the same time, there may be more restriction by exclusion than we realize. In 1946, when I was in high school, a Russian Communist was invited to address our weekly assembly. I remember that we were unconvinced by his protestations that the USSR wanted only peace. Afterwards students joked, "Yeah, a piece of Poland, a piece of Hungary and a piece of Germany." We were surprised to hear that the American Legion was upset that he had been allowed to speak to us. "What are they afraid of?" we thought. He hadn't captured our minds.

Some years later, after the Korean War, I heard a talk by a former American soldier who had been a prisoner of war and had gone over to the Chinese Communists. They had treated him well, given him a job, and even a daily glass of milk, which they understood to be necessary for Americans. But he found the conformity oppressive, became very homesick, and returned to the United States. He said he had been susceptible to their arguments because, coming from a small midwestern town, he had never heard the United States criticized and was impressed that some of their criticism was undeniably true.

Hearing this man, I realized he rebutted the American Legion's concern. Not having been exposed to dissident views, he had been a sitting duck for skillful propaganda; indeed, most of those who were similarly won over were from unsophisticated environments. I thought then how much we needed dissent.

Yet I doubt that many American high schools during the last three decades have invited a Communist to address their assembly. Since the McCarthy era we seem less tolerant of challenges to our basic political principles. The Socialist Party is all but nonexistent in America; political statements are tame and court the national consensus; free enterprise is not challenged. We pride ourselves on freedom of dissent but there is not much serious dissent in our politics, nor in the national media. Radical voices tend to be dismissed as lunatic. It's a free country, but we are as free to turn our backs on dissent as to express it.

In ordinary society, the cult processes of censorship and decreased contact with outsiders are often found, but in diminished intensity. Censorship of discordant information and isolation from heretical outsiders is usually done voluntarily rather than at the insistence of the group, although the expression of deviant views is seldom encouraged. Bankers tend to associate with bankers, doctors with doctors, sergeants with sergeants, black with black, and so on; similarly for various socioeconomic, ethnic, and religious groups. These associations provide not only shared interests, but also the security of support for one's views. Furthermore, liberals and conservatives tend to confine their reading to those magazines and columnists whose views are similar to their own; if they scan the writings of the opposition it will be to attack and disparage, not to learn. At political gatherings one seldom hears a serious questioning of the group's beliefs or any acknowledgement that opponents may be correct in a particular instance. Instead, what takes place is an exercise in mutual support and validation, a reinforcing of the group's belief in the correctness of its views, a strengthening of the fantasy of being true, good, and superior. A de facto censorship operates continuously. Whatever the cause of these social ghettos, their effect is to deny a person the benefit of being challenged and contradicted.

7 Escape from Cult Thinking

CULT BEHAVIOR IS PRESENT throughout society but is particularly evident in the military, whose fanatical support of the arms race has led us to the brink of extinction. The wish of military leaders for power and their training in destruction cause them to imagine enemies where there is none and to exaggerate the aggressive intentions of others. The military cult attempts to glorify war and is ready to sacrifice millions of lives for the abstraction of victory. Thus, generals and admirals are enthusiasts of nuclear weapons and think of them not much differently than the toy guns they fired gleefully as children—the bigger the better. For this reason, we must be aware of the influence and manipulation employed by the military establishment in order to maintain power and promote war. If we can see what is happening to us, we can take action to prevent them from leading us to nuclear disaster.

We are all susceptible to cult processes. Did you agree with what I said above about the military? I was purposefully devaluing them, using the same means that cults employ to define an outside group as evil. The attributions I made were exaggerated generalizations. Do you know any high-ranking military officers? It is possible that the paragraph above fits them, but most likely it does not.

Consider the phrase "the military, whose fanatic support of the arms race has led us to the brink of extinction." It permits no distinctions among members of the military, no recognition that opinions and motives vary from person to person, as in any other group. Such stereo-typing cannot account for statements such as this one on nuclear weapons:

> At the theatre or tactical level any nuclear exchange, however lim-ited it might be, is bound to leave NATO worse off in comparison to the Warsaw Pact, in terms both of military and civilian casualties and destruction. . . . To initiate use of nuclear weapons . . . seems to me to be criminally irresponsible.[1]

The person quoted is Field Marshall Lord Carver, Chief of the British Defense Staff from 1973 to 1976. He is not the only powerful military officer to take that position. Admiral Hyman Rickover, the principal force behind the development of the nuclear submarine fleet, on the occasion of his retirement, advocated doing away with nuclear weapons and nuclear reactors as well.

> The most important thing we could do is start by having an inter-national meeting where we first outlaw nuclear weapons, and then we outlaw nuclear reactors, too . . . I think it would be the finest thing in the world for the President of the United States to imme-diately initiate another disarmament conference . . . this is a very pro-pitious time, when the military expenses are eating up so much of the people's taxes.[2]

Nor is Rickover an exception among the American military. Gene LaRocque, another retired admiral, is a leading speaker for Physicians for Social Responsibility and heads the Center for Defense Informa-tion, a peace movement organization. And what are we to make of the fact that in May 1982 the entire Joint Chiefs of Staff supported reduc-tions in strategic nuclear arsenals in opposition to Secretary of Defense Caspar Weinberger, a civilian? Around the same time, the chairman of the Joint Chiefs supported the peace movement in its pressure for arms control. "Opponents of nuclear weapons in the United States 'are not a fringe element' but contain many who support a strong military and still want 'to get on with some arms control that is meaningful and results in very substantial reductions.'"[3] The military acted as a moderating force when the Joint Chiefs of Staff opposed President Reagan's wish to send a battleship group to South America.

My use of the term "fanatical" denigrates and devalues the opposing view by attacking the character of the opponent rather than addressing the content of what is proposed. A fanatic is "a person possessed by an excessive and irrational zeal, especially for a religious or political cause."[4] With the use of this term, advocacy of an arms buildup becomes "irrational zeal," without the writer having to prove that it is so. My demonstration paragraph contains no attempt to understand what legitimate basis might exist for the military's advocacy of an increased arms budget; that viewpoint is only condemned or devalued. The fact is, a general or an admiral might believe that a nuclear war would be an utter disaster for his or her country, but that an increased arms budget would help guard against such a war. And it is at least possible that such thinking might be correct. Some generals argue strongly for building up conventional forces rather than nuclear arms.

The sample paragraph given above does not acknowledge or discriminate among these possibilities. Instead, it attempts to establish a separate class of human beings, Them, characterized as wrong or bad—people not like Us. The reader is always included in the Us because in cult communication Us means good. We usually do not challenge such an inclusion even though its purpose is to exclude someone else, to lead Us to regard Them as bad or, at the least, inferior. This is a typical illustration of devaluation as it occurs in everyday life.

The second sentence of the paragraph establishes that the military has bad motives, "The wish of military leaders for power and their training in destruction causes them to imagine enemies where there is none and to exaggerate the aggressive intentions of others." Thus they want power and destruction and are paranoid to boot. The problem with this statement is projection. The sentence implies that the bad traits it designates characterize the military rather than anyone else, not the writer, and by unspoken agreement, not the reader. That implication is certainly false. A keen interest in violence and destruction can be found in almost everyone—witness the continued popularity of shoot-em-up, beat-em-up television and movie entertainment. In what seems to be the favorite plot, the villain has been so bad that the hero has license to behave brutally, cruelly, and vindictively, violating all precepts of fairness or legality in the process. Judging by the Neilson ratings, military personnel do not comprise the total audience for such bloodfests.

The capacity for violence, physical or psychological, is present in all human beings. At the same time, everyone thinks of him or herself as having good intentions. Indeed, after many years as a psychiatrist, it is clear to me that most human beings, especially those whose behavior is abhorrent, are likely to think of themselves as victims rather than villains, misunderstood by others, not appreciated, treated unfairly, not deserving the hardships encountered. It is doubtful that anyone rises in the morning exclaiming, "Aha! Another day to be evil!"

The wish for personal power is also universal and not confined to the military. As a liberal I have attended many peace movement meetings and have observed that being on a platform brings out the demagogue in many speakers and leaders, whether of the right, left, or center. I myself enjoy giving lectures to large groups of people and still remember one gathering of a thousand that responded with such enthusiasm that I could understand how Benito Mussolini must have felt when he spoke from his balcony. Power, vanity, and greed can flower exuberantly even while high-minded words are being declaimed. (I haven't attended any conservative or right-wing rallies but have observed them on television and read the speeches delivered there. The effect of the platform on the speaker is the same.)

The second sentence of our sample attributes a paranoid perspective to the generals and admirals ("to imagine enemies where there is none"). Quite possibly this does occur in the military, depending on the person and the circumstances, but this too is true of everyone else. Indeed, paranoia depends on attributing to some one or some group precisely those traits one denies in oneself, and the reader who accepted the opening paragraph did just that. The paragraph offers a good example of unnoticed, everyday projection, a basic cult dynamic. In this example the generals and admirals are the focus of projection, but just as often the peace movement, "doves," or "the Left" are designated as bad, inferior, irresponsible.

An interesting exercise is to consult the newspaper columnists, magazine authors, or television commentators who are your preferred sources of information and notice the devaluation and projection that is employed—with your tacit approval—when Washington politics, Russia, the Middle East, nuclear war, or other controversial subjects are discussed. The devaluation reinforces your sense of rightness and establishes a clear source of evil. Both Osama bin Laden and George W. Bush have made use of this tactic. Also observe the tone of righteousness that accompanies such cult thinking. It signals the presence of projection. They are bad and, therefore, We are good. You may notice in yourself the fantasy that if you were in power things would be done right!

The last two sentences of the chapter's opening paragraph sound a warning that is true enough ("we must be aware of the devices of influence and manipulation employed"), but that applies to everyone— the military, the peace movement, the Left and the Right, blacks and whites, Christians, Jews, and Muslims, rich and poor.

The military is authoritarian by nature and will inevitably manifest some of the cult behavior we have seen in religions, large corporations, and other social institutions. What is most important is that each of us becomes more aware of his or her own cult thinking. Only through such awareness can we extricate ourselves from the invisible, everyday cults of which we are members.

MY OWN (AND YOUR) CULT THINKING

The opening paragraph of this chapter was written to provide an experience of cult thinking by appealing to and stimulating the reader's likely prejudices, fears, and wishes. I used such a device because personal bias tends to make influence and manipulation invisible to those affected. If you are a member of the military or a hard-line conservative, you may not have been swayed; however, for many of us, characterizing generals and admirals as warmongering, stupid, or callous fits our projections very nicely. We consider ourselves, in contrast, to be peace-loving, intelligent, and empathic. We cannot grant laudable characteristics to people advocating very different views without raising the possibility that they could be correct and we in error.

Your response may be, "that's nothing new; I know all that." Indeed, the concept of cult behavior can be easily grasped, but experiencing it in one's own thinking and behavior is a different matter. Intellectuals in particular, who are trained not to be caught off balance by any idea, may find the concepts of cult psychology overly familiar and yet continue with their own cult behavior and be as ignorant of it as the members of Life Force. If you still feel immune from cult influence, I can offer a checklist of everyday behaviors that you may recognize all too well:

1. Speaking of adversaries or outsiders (e.g., conservatives, liberals, foreigners, rich, or poor) as if they were all the same; characterizing them by negative traits only; attributing unflattering motives to them but not to oneself.

2. Lacking interest and information concerning the actual statements and actions of opponents or outsiders.

3. Failing to consider the possible validity of an adversary's point of view.

4. Not taking a critical look at your own position.

5. Disapproving or rejecting a member of one's group for departing from the group position, devaluing the dissident, regarding him or her as an annoyance or a problem.

6. Feeling self-righteous.

OFFICIAL SELF-DECEPTION

Exit from the invisible cult is very important because cult thinking has such serious consequences, especially at the government level. In her book, *March of Folly,* Barbara Tuchman presents striking examples of both ancient and modern governments that persisted in disastrous policies while ignoring correct advice and countervailing experience. She blames this primarily on "wooden-headedness":

> Wooden-headedness, the source of self-deception, is a factor that plays a remarkably large role in government. It consists in assessing a situation in terms of pre-conceived fixed notions while ignoring or rejecting any contrary signs. It is acting according to wish while not allowing oneself to be deflected by the facts.[5]

We can recognize here a description of one of the basic cult behaviors, avoiding dissenting views. Correspondingly, in Tuchman's list of requirements for reasonable leadership we see the opposite—a readiness to learn, to acknowledge error:

> . . . to keep well-informed, to heed information . . . if the mind is open enough to perceive that a given policy is harming rather than serving self-interest, and self-confident enough to acknowledge it, and wise enough to reverse it.[6]

The only hope Tuchman sees for averting government folly is that the electorate be educated to select leaders by recognizing and rewarding integrity of character—moral courage—and rejecting "the ersatz." She is not sanguine about this possibility and concludes, somewhat helplessly, "We can only muddle on."

Actually, we are not that helpless. The study of cult psychology and its manifestations in ordinary life provides a framework with which to understand why wooden-headedness exists, what the behavior of a competent leader is, and how we can educate both leaders and electorate to do more than muddle on. The necessary information is available. If we allow ourselves the awareness of our wish for shepherds, our longing for the back seat of the car, then we have a much better chance of avoiding folly.

ILLUSORY DEBATES

The informed voter is supposed to be the bedrock of democracy, but an interesting study of citizen voting habits done in the 1950s suggests that the rational, objectively interested citizen does not really exist.[7] The researchers concluded that ill-informed, relatively indifferent voters are essential for a liberal democracy, and that only they are responsive to changing conditions, providing flexibility to the body politic. In contrast, well-informed, highly interested, involved citizens are usually quite partisan and unmoved by argument; on the Left and the Right, such stalwarts anchor the political ship, providing stability.

> Highly interested voters vote more, and know more about the campaign, and read and listen more, and participate more; however, they are also less open to persuasion and less likely to change. Extreme interest goes with extreme partisanship and might culminate in rigid fanaticism that could destroy democratic processes if generalized throughout the community.[8]

This somewhat disconcerting finding is due in part to the fact that what informs the citizen is largely propaganda issuing from one side or the other. Radio, television, magazines, and newspapers feature both critics and defenders of a particular policy, but each of these selects facts useful to his or her position, emphasizes certain principles and ignores others, often evoking emotional responses, prejudices, and fears. After reading or hearing such a presentation one may be persuaded, influenced, or won over. Nevertheless, if what one has encountered is not essential information but convincing propaganda, one is not really better informed.

Unless the audience knows a great deal about the subject, one-sided presentations can be very persuasive. In most conflict situations, disagreements are based on differences in interpretation and in the priorities given to different values; but these differences are seldom stated, and, lacking that clarification, we absorb highly selective information, are swayed to one side or the other, but end up no wiser.

As Jacques Ellul points out, whether propaganda is democratic or totalitarian does not matter, choice and discrimination are damaged:

> The existence of two contradictory propagandas is no solution at all . . . the individual is not independent in the presence of two combatants between whom he must choose. He is not a spectator comparing two posters, or a supreme arbiter when he decides in favor of the more honest and convincing one. . . . The individual is seized, manipulated, attacked from every side; the combatants of two propaganda systems do not fight each other, but try to capture him.[9]

Opposing propagandas do not assist the democratic process but produce partisans, each with the mind-set of a cult member who:

> . . . demands simple solutions, catchwords, certainties, continuity, commitment, a clear and simple division of the world into Good and Evil, efficiency, and unit of thought. He cannot bear ambiguity. He cannot bear that the opponent should in any way whatever represent what is right or good. . . . the individual will escape either into passivity or into total and unthinking support of one of the two sides.[10]

In order for the citizen to exercise a realistic choice a more searching alternative is needed, making use of dissent as a way of raising the level of informed judgment without raising the level of partisanship. Let us imagine a debate or discussion the goal of which is to clarify a controversial problem and proposed solutions. The focus would be on the fundamental questions of how the data are interpreted and what values are given priority. The intent would not be to overwhelm or capture the audience, but to clarify the competing values that are involved in the conflict and in the proposed solutions. In this way we could become informed without becoming opinionated. Logically, four areas would be clarified:

1. The key data. (Are they disputed?)

2. Interpretations of the data.

3. Value conflicts. (Reason for giving one value priority over the other?)

4. Error indicators. (What events or facts would indicate to each side that their belief or strategy should be changed?)

FOSTERING DISSENT

The best corporate executives promote real dissent even though they may find it irritating. Harold Geneen, who in the past ruled ITT like an absolute monarch, was nevertheless quite clear about the importance of dissent and said that he deliberately fostered it in his search for "the unshakeable facts":

> We cut through layers of fat in our management ranks by putting all the people in one room so they could talk with one another, face to face, regardless of rank, and an honest assessment of any situation could be based upon the facts which emerged.
>
> But that is only the surface of the matter. Beneath that surface was the clear understanding that we owed each other our honest opinions at all times. People could disagree with me or with anyone else; they could criticize me or anyone else, and no one would suffer as a consequence. I tried to welcome criticism. Naturally, no one likes to be criticized. One's first instinct is to be defensive and fight back. But that is the kind of defensiveness one should try to keep under control. I consciously tried to lean over backwards to avoid bridling when someone disagreed with me. I always wanted someone to point out where I might be heading for a mistake. I never batted down such a man. I listened and we exchanged views. . . . But more important than the encounter itself was that at meetings others observed what was happening and word got around the company that one could speak his mind, disagree with the boss, and be heard.[11]

Geneen's description of himself receives support from ITT executives whom Pascale and Athos interviewed:

"Geneen didn't mistrust people in a misanthropic sense," says one senior-level manager. "But he did mistrust a single source." Geneen disliked relying on one perspective as the means far giving him the whole picture. He believed that people have different points of view and that it is dangerous to listen to a small coterie.[12]

[Referring to the face-to-face confrontations that were encouraged at large executive meetings:] It was like a tennis match; you could play an aggressive game with your opponent but still have a relationship with him when their game was over.[13]

Jean Riboud, when CEO of Schlumberger, picked key people who were not afraid to disagree with him, people who had "the courage of their convictions," who did not "float like a cork," but "force[d] people to think." Ed Carlson, who was CEO of United Airlines, also valued dissent:

When Carlson was in accord with his advisors, he might play devil's advocate to see if he could support the opposite side with logic. "He sought the difference of opinion among his executives," said one observer, "and anyone in the group was expected to disagree loudly if he felt so disposed." Carlson's only rule: Disagree without being disagreeable.[14]

AN UNCOMFORTABLE PROCESS

Fostering dissent and recognizing its value are essential to realistic decision making. It is true that authoritarian decision-makers who dispense with dissent can be right in their decisions; but they can also be quite wrong. General Douglas MacArthur showed brilliant independent judgment during the Korean War in his insistence on an amphibious assault of Inchon despite the unanimous objections of the Joint Chiefs of Staff. In that case he was right. However, according to historian William Manchester, MacArthur's equally strong belief during World

War II that he would defeat the Japanese on the Lingayen beaches northwest of Manila led him to delay shifting vast stores of food and supplies to Bataan (as originally planned by the Joint Chiefs for a retreat and holding action). Finally, when it was too late to supply the peninsula, MacArthur retreated, but the troops, who otherwise would have been able to hold out for years, were starved into surrender and most died on the Death March.[15]

Today, nuclear weapons have made the stakes of government decision making higher than in the past. Only responsible dissent, voiced and listened to, can offer protection against cataclysmic error. With this need in mind, Irving Janis has suggested adopting procedures aimed at facilitating dissent in government. Among the steps he recommends are:

> Assign the role of critical evaluator to each member [of a policy-making group], encouraging the group to give high priority to airing objections and doubts.
>
> [The] setting up [of] several independent policy-planning and evaluation groups to work on the same policy question, each carrying out its deliberations under a different leader.
>
> One or more outside experts or qualified colleagues . . . who are not core members of the policy-making group should be invited to each meeting on a staggered basis and should be encouraged to challenge the views of the core members.
>
> At least one member should be assigned the role of devil's advocate.[16]

Janis recognizes the risks and difficulties in implementing his proposals, yet the steps outlined above would clearly be helpful in encouraging constructive dissent and lessening cult-like behavior at the highest levels of government. We can be confident that these procedures are practical because they have been used successfully already.

Following the Bay of Pigs disaster, President Kennedy sought to understand why his administration had blundered so badly, and when the next crisis occurred he put a much different system into operation.

In October of 1962, the discovery that the Soviet Union was installing nuclear missiles in Cuba spurred Kennedy to convene a group of high-level advisors to decide how to deal with the threat. Five of the key men selected had participated in the Bay of Pigs planning group: Rusk, McNamara, Dillon, Bundy, and Robert Kennedy. As before, they met under great time pressure, for they believed it was essential to take action before the missile sites became operational.

Rightly or wrongly, Kennedy ruled out a diplomatic approach. He made it clear that the situation was unacceptable and that the group task was to decide on the best form of coercive action to force the removal of missiles from Cuba.

This time, the team did not try to satisfy an impatient president by obtaining a quick consensus. They reacted quite differently, not only because they remembered what had happened at the Bay of Pigs, but because Kennedy saw to it that their deliberations took place under quite different procedures.

Each participant was expected to function as an independent critical thinker, addressing the problem in its entirety and not primarily as a spokesperson for the agency they represented. Robert Kennedy and Theodore Sorensen were given special roles to guard the group against superficial analysis. No formal agenda was imposed; discussions were free and far ranging. Outside experts were invited to give opinions and then were questioned closely. If visitors to the group remained silent, they were specifically asked to state their observations and comments. Sub-groups were formed to work independently on the same problem and then meet to compare findings. From time to time, President Kennedy absented himself from the group, especially in early phases when many different alternatives were first considered.[17]

As an example of the results of this different process, Robert Kennedy, who during the Bay of Pigs discussion had chided dissenters, this time guarded against premature closure of options. When an airstrike was proposed as the only option, he advised reconsideration. "'Surely,' he asserted, 'there was some course in between bombing and doing nothing.' . . . By the end of the first day of meetings the committee had seriously discussed at least ten alternatives."[18]

There was no false confidence, no shoving aside of the frightful risks that attended each option. The participants were encouraged to challenge each other's assumptions, to speak their minds frankly and treat each other, as well as outside visitors and consultants, as equals. Dissent was recognized as vital to finding a way to the most realistic action.

This process was often stressful for committee members, leading to unpleasant arguments, agitation, and sleepless nights. The discussions went on for days and seemed interminable, but in the end the blockade plan was decided upon. Furthermore, contingency plans were worked out in full detail to cope with a variety of possible Soviet responses. Nothing was taken for granted:

> As a result of the thorough review of *all the drawbacks* [emphasis added], the recommendations the group gave to the President included much more than strategic military guidelines. The group worked out in considerable detail ways of handling a variety of political, legal, and diplomatic ramifications, which, if neglected, could cause a blockade attempt to fail.[19]

The contrast to the Bay of Pigs deliberations is striking. Even if the blockade had not worked, the chances of success had been maximized and contingency responses were thought through and put in place. The practice of welcoming dissent—uncomfortable and disconcerting as it can be—proved immensely practical.

Unfortunately, it seems that presidents do not always learn from their predecessors. After the Tower report on the Iran-contra affair was released, Senator Nancy Kassenbaum, a Republican member of the Senate Foreign Relations Committee, commented:

> The underlying problem in all this is a lack of respect for dissent. The president has not been able to hear all sides of an issue. And we saw the same thing on SDI, contra aid, South Africa, and, of course, the budget. People in the administration who challenge policy are just shunted aside. That's the basic flaw in the process.[20]

THE EYE-LEVEL WORLD

Probably the most pervasive everyday cult behavior is devaluation of the outsider. As discussed earlier, we do this not only to feel superior, but also as a defense against recognizing those things in ourselves about which we feel ashamed and inferior; human beings tend to see someone else as embodying the defects they themselves deny. This projection of badness interferes with a realistic assessment of another's intentions. Frequently, it serves to justify violence. In contrast, an eye-level view recognizes defects and hurtful actions in the other without adopting a superior position or lowering the other to subhuman status.

In the service of realism, it is important to diminish projection and establish an eye-level perspective, for in our fears, hopes, and capacity for nobility as well as self-deception, we can recognize each other, see that "the enemy is us." Measures that reveal our similarities to the outsider not just our differences are very helpful. The reader may object that such perceptions of the hostile outsider must be mutual, that if we perceive the humanness and similarity of our enemies while they do not so perceive us, then we are at a fatal disadvantage. This is simply not so. Perceiving the other person without the distortion imposed by projection permits us to see more clearly, to respond more realistically. That response might be either aggressive or conciliatory, depending upon what is called for by the reality of the situation (not by the product of projective defenses). Such realism is always an advantage, especially in our dealings with other nations, other people, "the foreigner." At such times, cult behavior is likely to be most intense and mutual recognition most memorable.

Forty years after the Allied landing in France, an American soldier recalled that time:

> Arruda nodded, his hands touching the green napkin with its rough map of a 40-year-old battlefield. "I'd like to go back to the places I landed, the places I fought," he said, "to see the city of Cherbourg . . ."

And maybe he could find the spot in a field outside St. Lo where he stood up at the same time as a German officer who was only a few feet away.

"We looked at each other for the longest time, just staring," said Arruda. "I knew he had his troops behind him and he knew my people were back there. I was thinking, 'Hey, this son of a bitch is just like me.' And we both of us turned around very slowly and walked away from each other."[21]

GANDHI'S EXPERIMENT

Mahatma Gandhi was successful in achieving political change through non-violent civil disobedience. He served as a model for Kenneth Kaunda in Zambia, Martin Luther King in Montgomery, Alabama, and many others. Gandhi's principles of action were the opposite of cult behavior. He stressed putting oneself in the place of the opponent, respecting his or her potential goodness, and recognizing that you may be in error. Gandhi was quite explicit about what was required:

> I want you to feel like loving your opponents, and the way to do it is to give them the same credit for honesty of purpose which you would claim for yourself.
>
> . . . It is true that they have their ends to serve. But so have we our ends to serve. Only we consider our ends to be pure and, therefore, selfless. But who are we to determine where selflessness ends and selfishness begins?
>
> . . . Immediately we begin to think of things as our opponents think of them we shall be able to do them full justice.
>
> . . . Three-fourths of the miseries and misunderstandings in the world will disappear, if we step into the shoes of our adversaries and understand their standpoint.[22]

These principles directly combat devaluation and aim at establishing eye-level relationships that eliminate all self-righteousness. Gandhi went further and stressed that humiliation of the opponent was not permissible; great care was to be taken to maintain the opponent's dignity and self-respect. At every step Gandhi was concerned that the opponent save face, and this concern was a tribute to his realism. General Smuts remarked after experiencing Gandhi in South Africa. "It was my fate to be the antagonist of a man for whom even then I had the highest respect. . . . He never forgot the human background of the situation."[23]

Unfortunately, the vast majority of Gandhi's followers venerated him as a saint, to the detriment of the eye-level relationship he advocated in dealing with adversaries. They responded to him as to a parent ("Bapu"), with the dependency dynamics outlined for cults. As Erik Erikson's study made clear, Gandhi was quite capable of being authoritarian, tyrannical, and unjust to his own immediate family and disciples.[24] Everyone, even one called saint or genius, is flawed. The failure of Gandhi—like the failure of every great mass leader in human history—was not in having flaws, but in not freeing his followers from cult behavior. The awful violence between Moslims and Hindus that took place during his lifetime and afterward was a typical product of cult psychology. In the name of religions that advocate justice, mercy, generosity, and humility, the most barbarous atrocities were committed by each group against the other. Gandhi could stop them by fasting, but when Gandhi was gone most showed they had learned nothing.

DISTINGUISHING THE MORAL

Characteristically, cults subordinate ethical and moral standards to the particular aims of the group and leader. These are called higher purposes, usually put in terms of saving the world (as when the needs of Clara's child were made secondary to the needs of Life Force). In political situations in America, "saving the world for democracy," "overthrowing communism," "fighting terrorism," or the "war on drugs" are sometimes cited to justify illegal and immoral actions by the government. Undoubtedly, situations arise in which hard choices must be made; but often government officials use "higher purposes" to justify unsavory operations that are remarkably ineffective, if not disastrous:

the internment of the Japanese in 1942, the Bay of Pigs, the Tonkin Gulf incident, the bombing of Cambodia, the overthrow of Allende, and the sale of arms to Iran, among many others. Cult thinking is seldom realistic.

In contrast, the deliberations of the Cuban Missile Crisis planning group were guided by a basic approach strikingly consistent with Gandhi's, one which included concern for the ethics of any proposed action, putting oneself in the opponent's place and being careful to avoid humiliating him. The first days of the missile crisis group's discussions were occupied with the morality of an air strike against the Cuban bases. This proposal advanced by the military was at first favored by President Kennedy and Douglas Dillon. However, George Ball vigorously objected that such a surprise attack would be counter to our own traditions and harm our moral standing. Robert Kennedy agreed, pointing out the loss of innocent lives that would result and that such an action would be a "Pearl Harbor in reverse," going against our humanitarian ideals. Robert McNamara also agreed and in his retrospective account makes it clear that Robert Kennedy's stress on moral values was an important influence that resulted in the abandonment of the air strike option in favor of a blockade:

> His [Robert Kennedy's] contribution was far more than administrative . . . he opposed a massive surprise attack of a large country on a small country because he believed such an attack to be inhuman, contrary to our traditions and ideals and an act of brutality for which the world would never forgive us.[25]

In practice, realpolitik (which ignores ethical considerations) usually is cult-like in that it is linked to a devaluation of the enemy, to stereotyping and self-righteousness. In contrast, to understand and predict an opponent's actions, realism requires putting oneself in the opponent's place. In a Gandhi-like fashion, the Cuban Missile Group did just that:

> Most members viewed their opposite numbers in the Kremlin as no less rational than themselves. . . . Often the members of the group

set themselves the task of trying to predict how the enemy would react to one or another course of action by deliberately trying to imagine themselves in the Soviet leaders' place. . . . Without denying the cunning and deceit of the Soviet leaders, the group adopted the working assumption that the Soviet Union would not be likely to initiate a war unless unduly provoked. . . . Rusk and other members . . . urged the group to choose a response that the Soviet leaders could clearly see offered them a way out. . . . An important argument that led the group to regard a naval blockade as much more prudent than any alternative military response was precisely that this low-level action could serve as an unmistakable indication of America's strong intention to eliminate the missile bases without confronting the Soviet leaders with a belligerent act that would be "sudden or humiliating."[26]

Avoiding situations that would embarrass the Soviets was an important strategic consideration. Consequently, the first ship boarded was not Soviet, but a Lebanese freighter under charter to the Soviets. At every step, including American replies to Soviet proposals, care was taken to avoid provocative, unduly threatening, or humiliating actions.

Robert Kennedy concluded, "A final lesson of the Cuban missile crisis is the importance of placing ourselves in the other country's shoes."[27]

Gandhi would agree.

GOING BEYOND DEPENDENCE

Compliance with the group and dependence on a leader have served necessary functions in the survival of the human race. They are very important in childhood where they provide safety, security, encouragement, and support. Groups and leaders have legitimate functions for adults as well. They can stimulate, reinforce, and guide individuals' energies in constructive ways; they provide meaning and counter isolation and loneliness with acceptance and warmth. But the fantasy of parents must be transcended by adults; for us it is no longer functional. Indeed, regressive dependency makes our survival and progress more difficult because reality must be distorted in order to construct shepherds out of sheep.

Adult human beings stand together in a horizontal plane, but they all too often try to organize it vertically. The reader may assume that the eye-level world is his or her basic perspective. It hasn't been for me. Whenever I gave a public lecture I noticed that immediately afterward I felt let down, disappointed, no matter how well the audience had responded. Eventually, I realized that I was preparing my lectures as if the authority figures of my early professional years would be listening. At the periphery of my mind was an image of them seated in the back of the auditorium. There were no specific faces, just a row of skeptical shadows. I worked hard shaping and rehearsing my lectures to convince them of the rightness of my views, to win their approval, their grudging admiration. But when I stepped up on the platform and looked over the audience I could see that they weren't there. They hadn't come.

This fantasy of fathers, this vertical perspective, had been hidden from me until my disappointment alerted me to it. I know I am not alone in this. I can recognize the persistence of what I call the parent-world in the attitude and behavior of my friends, in the implicit views of authors whose books I read, and in the statements of public figures. As a psychotherapist, I find the parentworld in the fantasies of people with normal and useful adult positions—teachers, housewives, carpenters, lawyers, executives, students—people in all the occupations that comprise everyday society. The evidence is strong that all of us show the effects of having been raised in a hierarchical world in which there were those above us and those below. From such a perspective there is always a higher authority.

The child fears that the disappearance of parents would release anarchy, hatred, and destruction because in the parents' world the child knows no power, no control that is not imposed. In the eye-level world freedom is of a different kind, more responsible than before because the choices are your own, they are uncoerced and unbribed. "Free will is the experience of being the author of the law you obey." This world is different from that shaped by the dependency dream.

8 The Terrorist Threat

ONCE YOU START EXAMINING the features of cult thinking described in this book, you begin to recognize them in differing degrees in a wide variety of situations. Nevertheless, the quickest tip-off that something is amiss occurs when you see members of a group devalue outsiders while ignoring the faults of the leader and fellow believers. Outsiders—Them—are identified as inferior, bad, or damned. Those in the cult group—Us—are perceived as superior, good, or saved. We see this in its most extreme form in the mind of the terrorist.

Yet to think this way is to distort reality, for, in fact, human beings are not fundamentally different from each other. We know that when barriers are reduced or set aside, people see themselves in the Other. Indeed, this book is the result of seeing aspects of myself in others who had belonged to cults. As I listened to people recounting their cult histories at the research seminar I described in chapter one, they made me aware of the ubiquitous, everyday presence of cult behavior in people like myself who were not members of full-blown cults. Psychologically speaking, the abiding wish for security and protection makes the human race one family. Cult thinking says the opposite. If we keep this fact in mind, we can better understand terrorists and respond to their threats more realistically.

WHAT "THEY" THINK

Distinguished from the conventional violence of warfare, terrorism features the deliberate killing of civilians to coerce or intimidate a target group that goes beyond the victims of the attack. It is a sad fact that such terrorist acts have been perpetrated throughout history and in many parts of the world. Today everyone is aware that the United States is a target of a terrorist organization of worldwide scope called al Qaeda that is devoted to a holy war, a *jihad,* against Western powers, particularly the United States and Jews.

Most Westerners find themselves asking the question, "How could anyone devote themselves to the wholesale murder of innocent men, women, and children, and see this as a religious duty?" Although we have modern examples of slaughter for political and racist motives in the West—as in the case of Hitler and Stalin—we have to go back to the Crusades to find explicitly "holy" carnage. Nevertheless, the same fundamental cult behavior underlies the brutality and destruction evident in many political and religious movements; namely, devaluing the outsider. In the case of al Qaeda, the outsider is the non-Islamic West, the "infidel." Members of this rather large category are not only outsiders and different, but declared to be of the party of Satan, abhorred by Allah, damned. It is from this perspective that some teach that it is a religious duty on the part of Muslims to kill the infidel. With such an outlook, the September 11 suicide attack on the World Trade Center and the Pentagon is labeled a holy action of martyrdom. Not only is such martyrdom to be revered and honored, a sumptuous payoff is promised:

> A martyr's privileges are guaranteed by Allah; forgiveness with the first gush of his blood, he will be shown his seat in paradise, he will be decorated with the jewels of Imam [belief], married off to the beautiful ones, protected from the test in the grave, assured security in the day of judgment . . . wedded to seventy-two of the pure Houris [beautiful ones of paradise], and his intercession on behalf of seventy of his relatives will be accepted.[1]

What could better evoke wishes for reward and security—the dependency fantasy—discussed earlier in this book?

As in any cult, al Qaeda members' anger at their own exploitative and brutal governments is externalized and focused on a designated outsider. In this case evil Americans are the scapegoats for all their troubles and dissatisfactions. Certainly, the United States can be faulted. It has backed repressive, exploitative governments and embraced dictators when it seemed expedient despite the violation of democratic standards and values. On the other side, extreme brutality is commonly employed by Islamic states. But typical of cult thinking, the critical gaze of al Qaeda is turned away from examples of Islamic nations' violations of human rights and their own responsibility for failing to match the prosperity of the West. To do so would disrupt the fantasy of being the good Us (we of Islam), in contrast to the bad Them (they of the West).

Moreover, terrorism as a political or religious weapon is not endorsed in the traditional teachings of Islam. Though established with the goal of creating governments throughout the Middle East operating according to strict Islamic law, its leader, Osama bin Laden, uses carefully selected passages in the Koran and devious reasoning to justify killing women and children—something explicitly forbidden by Mohammed. Rohan Gunaratna, a terrorism expert who has done extensive research on al Qaeda, puts the matter succinctly: "In effect, contemporary Islamists such as al-Zuwahiri and Osama are engaged in an unprecedented exercise of corruption, misinterpreting and misrepresenting the word of God to generate support for their political mission."[2]

Nevertheless, as in the case of less spectacular, but no less violent domestic cults, religious war offers many psychological benefits. Mark Juergensmeyer, a professor of sociology at the University of California, Santa Barbara, sagaciously observes:

> To live in a state of war is to live in a world in which individuals know who they are, why they have suffered, by whose hand they have been humiliated. . . . Perhaps most important, it holds out hope of victory and the means to achieve it. In the images of cosmic war this victorious triumph is a grand moment of social and personal trans-

formation, transcending all worldly limitations. One does not easily abandon such expectations. To be without such images of war is
almost to be without hope itself.[3]

Ironically, it is a common theme of terrorist groups, domestic and
foreign, that it is they who are the victims. Victimization is a theme
taken up and amplified by the terrorist. Thus we find bin Laden asserting that because of U.S. actions in the Middle East, it was America
that declared war on the Muslim world.

Juergensmeyer points out further that a process of devaluation, or
"Satanization" in the language of al Qaeda, sets the stage for a cosmic
war and an end to humiliation

> As we have seen, the idea of cosmic war is compelling to religious
> activists because it ennobles and exalts those who consider themselves
> a part of it—especially those who have been desperate about their
> situations and defiant in resisting them. In that sense the conflict is
> not just an effort at delegitimization but at dehumiliation: it pro-
> vides escape from humiliating and impossible predicaments for those
> who otherwise would feel immobilized by them. They become in-
> volved in terrorism not only to belittle their enemies but also to pro-
> vide themselves with a sense of power.[4]

The attraction of such a fantasy of ultimate salvation was seen in the
guru cults that flourished in the United States in the 1960s and 1970s,
as exemplified by the Life Force group described earlier. Large numbers of disciples looked to "enlightened" masters who could provide
answers that would give their lives direction and meaning, culminat-
ing in union with divine purpose. Some went on to make headlines via
their own version of martyrdom. The Branch Davidians at Waco, Texas,
led by David Koresh, and the Peoples Temple at Jonestown, Guyana,
led by Jim Jones, were lurid examples of violence turned against the
members at the behest of religious leaders. Members of the Aum cult
in Japan released poison gas in the Tokyo subway as part of a strategy
of killing all outsiders to prepare the world for a new order.[5]

A striking example of Them-and-Us psychology can be seen in the fact that the perception of what constitutes an act of terror depends on who is doing it. Some idea of this cult-like selective vision can be gained by considering a poll conducted among Palestinians in December 2001. As reported by Gail Luft in *Foreign Affairs* magazine:

> More than 94 percent of Palestinians told pollsters that they viewed Israeli incursions into Area A as acts of terror, while 82 percent refused to characterize the killing of 21 Israeli youths outside a Tell Aviv disco six months earlier that way. . . . only 41 percent of Palestinians . . . viewed the September 11 attacks as terrorism. And 94 percent reported that they would characterize a hypothetical Israeli use of chemical or biological weapons against Palestinians as terrorism, whereas only 26 percent would say the same about Palestinian use of those weapons against Israel.[6]

The Islamic media does not counter this distorted perception. Opposition to the inflamed rhetoric of "the street"—to the extent that it exists—is not expressed publicly. The media in Egypt and Saudi Arabia, regimes ostensibly friendly to the United States, put out virulent anti-American and anti-Jewish polemics. Apparently their governments find it useful to stimulate the wrath and violence of extremist groups, exploiting group compliance and directing the anger of the populace away from themselves. Indeed, voices of moderation are reviled. Thus, not only is the cult behavior of devaluation involved, compliance with the group and avoiding dissent is taking place consciously and unconsciously in various Islamic states where dissent can result in death, not just disapproval.

Loss of realism is the price of cult behavior no matter on whose side it occurs. Believing the United States lacked the will to fight because it had left areas such as Somalia when violence threatened its soldiers, bin Laden was betrayed by his devaluation of U.S. resolve. Undoubtedly, bin Laden's wish—and need—to feel superior to the infidel played a part in his misreading of the United States. That loss of realism became clear when, in response to September 11, the United States sent troops to Afghanistan, destroyed bin Laden's training camps, and ousted the

Taliban. According to Gunaratna and other experts, bin Laden hadn't expected such a swift and all-out response. He had decided that Americans—unlike the Islamic faithful—were unwilling to risk the lives of their soldiers. Saddam Hussein made a similar miscalculation based on devaluation when he believed the United States would not have the stomach for urban warfare in Baghdad.

WHAT "WE" THINK

But it is not enough to recognize the cult aspects of al Qaeda, it is important that we all become aware how cult thinking affects our responses. Another example of the cost of unrecognized cult thinking is apparent in the case of the U.S. government's refusal to recognize the connection between the extreme behavior of cults, such as the Branch Davidians of Waco, Texas, and the less obvious cult tendencies of our own familiar religions. The FBI devalued the Davidians as if it were a criminal organization—not as a religious group with a leader worshipped by disciples. Had the FBI been more willing to label the group a religion, albeit one with a self-righteously grandiose leader, it might have sought out an appropriate religious leader to talk with David Koresh and work out a religion-based rationale for a solution that didn't end in the group's immolation. Instead, it employed an assault team to "rescue" the "hostages." I suspect this reluctance to categorize the Branch Davidians as a religious group also may have prevented the FBI from seeing that Koresh would never submit to an inglorious conclusion to his story and that his followers would obey him even to the point of losing their own lives.

At the time, national media displayed a similar reluctance to draw parallels between the Branch Davidians and mainstream groups. During the Waco siege and its aftermath, I was interviewed a number of times by news programs as an expert on cult psychology. On two of those occasions, I pointed out that the behavior of some anti-abortion groups in harassing patients and staff of abortion clinics—which culminated in murders of staff and numerous bombings of clinics—

reflected cult thinking not fundamentally different than what had taken place among the Davidians. These comments were edited out and did not appear during the broadcasts of the interviews. Indeed, many people even today would be hesitant to call the perpetrators of "pro-life" violence terrorists, though similar thinking is promoted by al Qaeda with much the same religious fervor.

Being able to recognize cult thinking at work in our own backyard is becoming increasingly important. Fundamentalist groups that devalue the outsider and avoid or punish dissent are on the rise all over the world. Yet despite the fact that the worst violence against human beings has been committed by self-righteous people citing God as their authority—al Qaeda being perhaps one of the most remarkable examples—we avoid scrutinizing followers of religions in our own backyard with the same critical eye we cast on those whose religious form is in some way alien.

Consider a news report by Alan Cooperman for the *Washington Post* in July of 2002:

> A high-ranking Lutheran pastor has been suspended from his duties and ordered to apologize to all Christians for participating with Muslims, Jews, Sikhs, and Hindus in an interfaith prayer service in Yankee Stadium after September 11. The Missouri Synod's national second vice president, Reverend Wallace Schultz wrote in the suspension letter: '. . . a crystal clear signal was given to others watching the event and to C-Span. The signal was: While there may be differences as to how people worship or pray, in the end, all religions pray to the same God. . . . To participate with pagans in an interfaith service and, additionally, to give the impression that there might be more than one God, is an extremely serious offence against the God of the Bible.'

Notice that "pagans" is used to categorize Muslims, Jews, Sikhs, and Hindus. From the point of view of the Reverend Schultz, they are clearly the Outsider and of lesser value.

While no official body suppresses dissenting views in the United States where the First Amendment protects freedom of speech and the press, there is nevertheless a de facto censorship that deprives citizens of the wide range of political thinking needed to address complicated problems. As described earlier, when journalism scholar Ben H. Bagdikian wrote *The Media Monopoly* in 1982, he stated with alarm that "fifty corporations own most of the output of daily newspapers and most of the sales and audience in magazines, broadcasting, books, and movies."[7] Today, fifteen years later, he reports that media control is in the hands of only six corporations—giant conglomerates that reflect the interests of the advertisers that supply most of their income. With such a concentration of power, problems attendant to conflicts of interest are bound to arise. How complete and objective can news reporting and analysis be if it is likely to arouse the ire of those who provide most of the media's income? Such a narrowing of conceptual options hampers attempts to find realistic solutions to major problems. But the principal contribution this makes to cult thinking is in the way it perpetuates and intensifies the disjunction between Them and Us by slanting, selecting, and omitting information that would lessen the divide.

We would do well to see that the fantasy of the cosmic war, of Good combating Evil in accordance with God's Will, can seduce us as well as al Qaeda. We, too, are susceptible to the attraction of the Holy War in its many forms, so well described by Juergensmeyer:

> Insofar as the scenarios of cosmic war is a story, it carries a momentum toward its completion and contains the seeds of hope for its outcome. I use the term *hope* rather than *fear*, for no one wants to believe in a story that cannot produce a happy ending. Those who accept that their life struggles are part of a great struggle, a cosmic war, know that they are part of a grand tale that will ultimately end triumphantly, though not necessarily easily or quickly. The epic character of the story implies that the happy ending may indeed be long delayed—perhaps until after one's lifetime or after the lifetimes of one's descendents.[8]

Such a stance ended up pervading the Life Force psychology group described earlier.

We hear echoes of the holy war mentality in comments made here in the United States. Consider the following statement and guess its source:

> This is an historic moment. . . . You have a mission. It is almost a divine mission. You have one task in life. That is to wage a global campaign against terrorism and weapons of mass destruction. . . . It is a noble, wonderful mission. Our children's lives will be better for it. You are given the opportunity by tragedy to solve the larger problem. It is virtually impossible to wipe out terrorist groups, but, by God, you can wipe out countries that support terrorism.

These were comments made by Kenneth Adelman, a former head of the Arms Control and Disarmament Agency under Ronald Reagan. Adelman was replying to the question put to him by the *New Yorker* writer Nicholas Lernam as to what he would say to President Bush if he had the chance.[9]

Adelman makes no mention of why the United States is hated in the Middle East. That hatred has different causes, some of which amount to envy, displaced anger, and feelings of failure on the part of Middle Eastern citizens. But the hatred also results from a foreign policy that is perceived as arrogant, selfish, and hypocritical. One example is the belief that the United States has not been even-handed in dealing with the Israeli/Palestinian conflict. As Malise Ruthven, Islamic scholar and expert on the Middle East, summarizes the contradictions of the current U.S. position:

> A policy which attacked systemic human rights violations in Iraq whilst implicitly defending them (by arming the government and by not condemning violations) in the Israel-occupied territories and Saudi Arabia is certain to fail in the long term.[10]

President Bush has said not a word about such issues, and, consequently, the United States is seen as refusing to acknowledge its errors and continuing to pursue policies antithetical to its stated beliefs. This profound silence about such criticisms, and the lack of information about other options, constitutes a considerable avoidance of information that otherwise could reduce the gap between Them and Us. This avoidance continues despite the ill will it engenders and the distorting influence it has on foreign policy. Devaluation thrives on the absence of accurate and balanced information. As a consequence, just as bin Laden underestimated the American response to September 11, we are likely being unrealistic in analyzing Middle Eastern problems and possible solutions.

The fantasy of the holy war, the Good versus the Bad, the Saved versus the Damned, influences U.S. foreign policy more than many people realize. Since the Oslo Accords, followed by the Saudi proposal of land-for-peace, and more recently President George W. Bush's roadmap for peace, it is not only Hamas that has balked at possible solutions, but in the United States, a coalition of fundamentalist Christians and ultra-Orthodox Jews have been a potent political force opposed to any land transfer. Similar to Islamists insisting on a literal reading of the Koran to advance their millennial hopes, both of these groups base their opposition on their reading of the Bible.

For many evangelical Christians the return of the Jews to Palestine and Jerusalem is a sign of the "End Times," representing a fulfillment of prophecy and a prelude to Armageddon and the Rapture. These events, they believe, are predicted in the Book of Revelations and precede the return of Christ when faithful Christians (and converted Jews) rise up to Heaven and are saved. For their part, the ultra-Orthodox Jews believe they must occupy all the biblical lands for the Messiah to appear. Therefore, the West Bank must be settled and no Palestinian territory can be relinquished.

It remains to be seen how, or if, these conflicting totalistic worldviews can be resolved, or what role the United States might play in creating a solution. Yet resolving the Israeli-Palestinian conflict would be a potent weapon in combating terrorism because it would eliminate what at present is a refueling station for intense anger at the United States.

Compliance with the group may often be a conscious political decision, but there are indications that pressure for compliance—as in a typical cult—can unconsciously affect the government agencies that supply the information used to make strategic decisions. Former Congressman Lee Hamilton, who for thirty-four years served on numerous intelligence committees, commented on the Iraq situation prior to the U.S. invasion: "The whole intelligence community knows exactly what the president wants and most are in their jobs because of the president—certainly the people at the top—and they will do everything they can to support the policy."[11]

LOOKING FOR CAUSES

Like most other experts on Islamic affairs, Gunaratna stresses that in addition to a strong military and police response, it is of equal importance to work at

> . . . resolving Kashmir, Palestine, and other international conflicts where Muslims are affected; redressing grievances and meeting the legitimate aspiration of Muslims; and helping Arab and Muslim states to improve the quality of life of their citizens. Above all, al Qaeda's ideology must be countered, in order to deflect and lessen its appeal to serving members, fresh recruits and actual or potential supporters.[12]

Robert J. Lifton came to a similar conclusion after his study of the Aum cult of Japan: ". . . even as we insist upon holding people responsible for their actions, we desperately need to explore ways in which to alter the psychological and historical conditions so conducive to the kinds of destructiveness and evil in which Aum engaged."[13]

The motivations of the terrorists are diverse, as are their educational and social backgrounds. However, a certain picture does emerge. Ruthven cites Paul Pillar of Brookings Institute, who describes the majority of terrorists as: ". . . worldly-wise young adult males, unemployed or underemployed (except by terrorist groups), with weak social and familial family support and with poor prospects for economic improvement and advancement through legitimate work."[14]

In contrast, Daniel Pipes, director of the Middle East Forum, suggests that, "like fascism and Marxism-Leninism in their heydays, militant Islam attracts highly competent, motivated, and ambitious individuals. Far from being the laggards of society, they are its leaders."[15] He cites other researchers who found that economic factors did not seem to be an important motivator and quotes Princeton historian Sean Wilentz' ironic observation that "terrorism is caused by 'money, education and privilege.'" Similarly, Palestinian journalist Khalid M. Amayreh observed that "A substantial majority of Islamists and their supporters come from the middle and upper socio-economic strata."[16] I suggest further that it is not deprivation or injustice that is the decisive motivation for terror, but the need to see oneself as good and heroic, esteemed by the community and blessed by God. Terrorism makes it possible for men and women to see themselves as noble warriors, restoring honor to Islam. It has been remarked that the basic human instinct is not self-preservation but preservation of the self-image. The *jihad* solves that problem. We must not forget it in dealing with other countries, especially in the Middle East. Surely that need for self-respect—despite the horrific means chosen to achieve it—is not dissimilar to our own.

LOOKING FOR SOLUTIONS

What can we do about terrorism in general and al Qaeda in particular? There is no simple answer to a problem that reflects economic, theological, political, and criminal aspects. The first step is to recognize and address the different populations involved in the problem. Specifically, in addition to the committed al Qaeda terrorist there are those who support the terrorist cause or, at the least, are sympathetic to it, but do not actively participate in terrorist actions. Then there are those who oppose terrorist activity, but are intimidated by "the street" and are silent. A few dare to speak in direct opposition.

Committed terrorists cannot be readily dissuaded or negotiated with; they are not willing to compromise because they deal in absolutes and, cult-like, fiercely reject any doubts raised as to the righteousness of their actions. Such people must be deterred, intercepted, imprisoned. Alan

Dershowitz, professor at Harvard Law School, makes a compelling case for not rewarding terror by negotiations or concessions. Otherwise, the leadership will feel—and they have made statements to that effect— that terrorist activities have been their most successful means of influencing the international community and should be increased to achieve their goals.[17] But the local environment that provides new recruits for al Qaeda can be affected by supplying corrective information to counter the misinterpretation promulgated in the religious school and the militant media. It is this group that should be the focus of our remedial efforts. Unless that is done, there is no end in sight to the conflict, only an escalation.

Corrective information also is important to expose the fantasies about suicide bombers, both in the Middle East and other sympathetic countries. The suicide bomber is presented as heroic by al Qaeda and its sympathizers. We need to recognize that for many the sacrifice is heroic, if misguided. Human beings have a limitless capacity to rationalize their behavior. When such rationalizations are supported by the community, they are even harder to counter. Killing innocent civilians becomes a noble act to the suicide bomber who has been told it is a religious duty. Some Islamic authorities are quite aware of this problem of spurious religious authorization and have issued *fatwa* opposing suicide terror tactics. After Shi'ite Shaikh Muhammad Hussein Fadlallah, spiritual leader of Hizbollah in Lebanon, declared suicide bombing contrary to Islamic law, Shi'ite suicide bombings in Lebanon ceased.[18] Further intervention by Islamic religious authorities would be very important in confronting the abuse of religious doctrine. As it stands now, terrorist cult thinking is supported and intensified by governments in such countries as Egypt, Saudi Arabia, and Syria, where articles in government-supported media call for the extermination of Americans and Jews.

But there is an opportunity for combating al Qaeda's cult thinking that is seldom mentioned: the cultivation in the Middle East of independent news and commentary. We have seen that dissent offers a powerful correction to cult distortions. Repeatedly, members of cults—such as Hugh and Clara—were able to escape their ideological confinement when they were able to make contact with former cult members who had become disillusioned with the leader. In other instances, reading or hearing dissenting views and counter arguments made exit from the cult possible. So it is not surprising that cult-like groups make use of censorship, selection, and omission of information to keep their point of view persuasive.

Following up on this insight might suggest the West should institute a massive propaganda assault to "capture" minds in the Middle East. But the problem is complicated. David Hoffman, president of Internews Network, Inc., writing in *Foreign Affairs* magazine, argues against such a tactic and, instead, proposes that the United States do everything it can to support independent local media, whether favorable to the United States or not. He believes that propaganda via Voice of America (VOA) broadcasts would only arouse resentment and suspicion, and:

> . . . even when effective, . . . leave no rudimentary foundations in place on which the democratization of Arab and Muslim societies can begin. . . . The best way for Washington to reverse the tide in the propaganda war," he argues, "is to support those forces in the Muslim community that are struggling to create modern democracies and institutionalize the rule of law. That the majority of the Muslim world disagrees with many aspects of U.S. policy does not preclude those same people from also craving more independent and pluralistic media based on Western-style objective journalism.[19]

The hunger for actual news to which Hoffman alludes is illustrated by the fact that thirty independent television channels and eleven independent radio stations have been started in the West Bank. The most popular television news service in the Middle East is the independent station al-Jazeera. In Europe we have had examples of independent media being vital in weakening the grip of autocratic regimes. For example, in Czechoslovakia the wide dissemination of homemade videotapes of soldiers and police beating students was crucial in the Czech uprising against Russian rule. Students took the videotapes into the countryside and showed the rural population what was actually happening in the cities. In the Balkans, independent radio and television stations were major forces helping the democratic opposition to Milosevic. In some places, attempts by local authorities to close down media were met with crowds of protestors who finally prevailed and reopened the stations. Hoffman concludes: "If experience in non-Muslim countries is any indication, well-produced, objective, indigenous journalism will get higher ratings than either exhortative reports from state news organs or more distant news from satellite broadcasters. Ultimately, audience will always drive the media."[20]

Studies of cult psychology point exactly in this direction. Groups like al Qaeda rely on restricted information for recruiting new members. Most children and young men in the Middle East have received little education except to study and recite the Koran; the women even less. Those who gain advanced degrees in engineering or other hard sciences have been narrowly focused and are naïve about history and the realities of democracy and modernity. Even residing in the United States may be viewed through the distorting lens supplied by al Qaeda. It is telling that Mohammed Atta, who directed the September 11 attack, during his stay in the United States saw only the caricatures portrayed on television and the underbelly of urban life.

In promoting independent local media, regardless of their political or religious outlook, we would be countering al Qaeda's propaganda while relying on the human qualities that reverberate with the choice we offer, people's wish for freedom. Freedom is our strong suit, and objective information is its most telling manifestation. Diversity of views and open discussion undermines cult control and provides a basis for representative government.

More independent media voices are needed in the United States, as well as abroad, to combat the devaluing of the Other. This book shows how such devaluation is a basic cult dynamic that supports violence against the innocent and legitimizes terror. In turn, devaluation requires misinformation and distortion so that the Other is perceived as malignant, deserving extermination—definitely Not Me. Dependence on a leader and compliance with the group, the two cult behaviors so evident in the history of Hugh and Clara, are the means whereby devaluation and misinformation are initiated. Avoiding dissent enables misinformation to be maintained. In the case of religion-based terror, the wish for the security of an all-powerful, rewarding parent-God motivates violent actions that violate core religious teachings. We saw how that occurred to Hugh and Clara in Life Force. The high ideals with which they started were gradually subverted until they ended up acting in ways that violated the moral principles in which they had believed.

Cult thinking is basic to all human beings because of our childhood dependence on parents. Although later as adults we have at our disposal much more sophisticated mental capacities, we carry with us a heritage of dependency: the vision and hope for a super family providing the security of the back seat of the car. This longing, portrayed with so much charm in the PEANUTS© cartoon in chapter one, can lead to terribly destructive results beginning with the perception of other humans as Them. Them is the enemy, so they cannot be Good, as we are. We blame Them, hate Them, exploit Them, and kill Them. The irony is that we are all Them to someone else. Currently, we are Them to al Qaeda, and They want to kill Us. Can we be realistic in our response to this threat? Can we avoid devaluing al Qaeda as they do us, selecting facts to support our own fantasy of being Good, unlike Them? A more realistic view may seem to offer less security than does fantasy, but actually it offers more. If we allow ourselves to see our own fantasies, we too can exit from cult thinking and respond to terrorism more effectively.

CODA

From a larger perspective, it may be that our struggle to deal with the terrorist threat could make clear the danger inherent in any ideology, any system of belief offering utopian goals at the cost of compliance, conformity, and the suppression of dissent. The warning sign of ideology is the sharp division between Them and Us, whether it is based on politics, economics, race or religion. The possibilities for destruction and misery endemic to such beliefs have been multiplied many times by modern science. As a result, the few can now destroy the many, and that power is becoming increasingly accessible. I hope the danger may cause us to recognize that we all share the same needs for meaning, security, and a positive future. From that point of view we are one family. Understanding this fundamental fact is the antidote to cult thinking.

There is no Them. There is only Us.

Notes

INTRODUCTION

1. Robert Jay Lifton, *Thought Reform and the Psychology of Totalism* (New York: W. W. Norton, 1969).

CHAPTER 1: THE CULT MIRROR

1. Seminar sponsored by the Center for the Study of New Religious Movements, in Berkeley, California, 1980–81.

CHAPTER 3: COMPLIANCE WITH THE GROUP

1. For a convincing analysis of this in French society see Pierre Bourdieu, *Distinction: A Social Critique of the Judgment of Taste* (Cambridge, Mass.: Harvard University Press, 1984).

2. The analyst is quoted in Janet Malcolm, *Psychoanalysis: The Impossible Profession* (New York: Alfred Knopf, 1981), p. 53.

3. Robert B. Cialdini, *Influence—Science and Practice* (Glenview, Illinois: Scott, Foresman and Company, 1985), pp. 101–2.

4. Ibid., p. 98.

5. Sigmund Freud, "Group Psychology and the Analysis of the Ego," in *The Standard Edition of the Complete Psychological Works of Sigmund Freud,* ed. J. Strachey (London: The Hogarth Press, 1955), vol. 18, p. 76.

6. Ibid., pp. 122–123.

7. Ibid., pp. 124–125.

8. Margaret Rioch, "The Work of Wilfred Bion on Groups" in Arthur D. Colman and W. Harold Bexton, *Group Relations Reader* (Sausalito, California: GREX, 1975), p. 24.

9. Arthur D. Colman, "Group Consciousness as a Developmental Phase," Ibid., pp. 35–42.

10. Rosabeth Kanter, *Commitment and Community: Communes and Utopias in Sociological Perspective* (Cambridge, Mass.: Harvard University Press, 1972), p. 87.

11. Ibid., p. 88.

12. Alfons Heck, *A Child of Hitler: Germany in the Days When God Wore a Swastika* (Frederick, Colorado: Renaissance House, 1985).

13. Lowell Streiker, *The Gospel Time Bomb: Ultrafundamentalism and the Future of America* (Buffalo, New York: Prometheus Books, 1984), p. 81.

14. Ibid., p. 81.

15. See Walter Hilton, *The Scale of Perfection* (London: Burns & Oates, 1953), pp. 14–15; St. John of the Cross, *The Complete Works of St. John of the Cross* (Westminster: Newman Press, 1953) vol. 1, p. 457; and Philip Kapleau, *The Three Pillars of Zen* (Boston: Beacon Press, 1967), p. 40.

16. Diane Margolis, *The Managers: Corporate Lip in America* (New York: Murrow, 1979), pp. 107–09.

17. Quoted in Ibid., p. 52.

18. Quoted in Ken Auletta, *The Art of Corporate Success: The Story of Schlumberger* (New York: Viking Penguin, 1984), pp. 131–132.

19. Rosabeth Kanter, *Men and Women of the Corporation* (New York: Basic Books, 1977), p. 110.

20. Quoted in Richard Pascale and Anthony Athos, *The Art of Japanese Management: Applications for American Executives* (New York: Warner Books, 1981), p. 115.

21. Margolis, pp. 107, 109.

22. Richard Pascale, "The Paradox of 'Corporate Culture': Reconciling Ourselves to Socialization" (Research Paper No. 738, Stanford University 1984, Graduate School of Business), p. 5.

23. Pascale and Athos, p. 286.

24. Pascale, p. 6–7.

25. Quoted in Barbara Underwood and Betty Underwood, *Hostage to Heaven* (New York: Clarkson Potter, 1979), p. 70.

26. Margolis, pp. 62–63.

27. Auletta, p. 161.

28. Quoted in Ibid., pp. 123–124.

29. Terrance Deal and Allen Kennedy, *Corporate Cultures: The Rights and Rituals of Corporate Life* (Reading, Mass.: Addison-Wesley 1982) p. 195.

30. Thomas Peters and Robert Waterman, Jr., *In Search of Excellence: Lessons from America's Best-Run Companies* (New York: Warner Books, 1982), p. 78.

31. Pascale and Athos, p. 320.

32. Paul Brodeur, "The Asbestos Industry on Trial," *New Yorker*, 10, 17, and 24 June 1985.

33. Morton Mintz, *At Any Cost: Corporate Greed, Women and the Dalkon Shield* (New York: Pantheon, 1986).

34. Margaret Rioch, "'All We Like Sheep—': Followers and Leaders," in Colman and Bexton, p. 170.

CHAPTER 4: DEPENDENCE ON A LEADER

1. Craig Karpel, "The Gnomes of Bilderberg," *Penthouse*, May 1981, p. 152.

2. Ibid.

3. James Barber, *New York Times*, 26 April 1984, p. 25.

4. Rioch, "'All We Like Sheep—,'" p. 159.

5. Investigative Poetry Group, *The Party: A Chronological Perspective on a Confrontation at a Buddhist Seminary* (Woodstock, New York: Poetry, Crime and Culture Press, 1977), p. 55.

6. Ibid., p. 56.

7. Quoted in Gary Wills, *Reagan's America*, (New York: Penguin Books, 1988), p. 355.

8. Peters and Waterman, Jr., p.84.

9. Harold Geneen (with A. Moscow), *Managing*, (Garden City, New York: Doubleday, 1984), p. 144.

10. Quoted in J. Patrick Wright, *On a Clear Day You Can See General Motors* (New York: Avon, 1979), p. 68.

11. Peters and Waterman, Jr., pp. 31, 46, 48.

12. Erich Fromm, *Escape From Freedom* (New York: Farrar & Rinehart, 1941).

13. Peters and Waterman, Jr., p. 68.

14. Cornelle Meier, interview with the author, 11 June 1986.

15. Christopher Byron, *The Fanciest Dive* (New York: Norton, 1986), p. 103.

16. Quoted in Margolis, p. 93.

17. Craig Lambert, *Harvard Magazine,* September-October 2002, pp. 40–41.

18. Saint John of the Cross. *The Complete Works of Saint John of the Cross.* Westminister: Newman Press, 1953.

19. Quoted in Flo Conway and Jim Siegelman, *Holy Terror: The Fundamentalist War on America's Freedoms in Religion, Politics, and Our Private Lives* (New York: Dell, 1982), p. 283.

20. R. Knight, "Determinism, 'Freedom,' and Psychotherapy," *Psychiatry,* 9 (1946), pp. 251–62.

21. Idries Shah, *The Dermis Probe* (London: Octagon Press, 1980), p. 158.

22. Joan Chittister, "No Time for Tying Cats," in *Midwives of the Future,* ed. Ann Ware (Kansas City, Missouri: Leaven Press, 1985), p. 7.

23. Quoted in Conway and Siegelman, p. 234.

24. James Kavanaugh, *A Modern Priest Looks at His Outdated Church* (New York: Trident Press, 1967), p. 178.

25. Liz Harris, "Holy Days," *New Yorker,* 30 September 1985, p. 92.

26. Barbara Underwood and Betty Underwood, *Hostage to Heaven* (New York: Clarkson Potter, 1979).

27. Quoted in Conway and Siegelman, p. 252.

28. Arthur J. Deikman, "Comments on the GAP Report on Mysticism," *Journal of Nervous and Mental Disease,* 165:3 (1977), pp. 213–217.

29. Arthur J. Deikman, *The Observing Self: Mysticism and Psychotherapy* (Boston: Beacon Press, 1982).

30. Arthur J. Deikman, "The Evaluation of Spiritual and Utopian Groups," *Journal of Humanistic Psychology,* 23:3 (1983), pp. 8–19.

31. Idries Shah, *The Way of the Sufi* (London: Jonathan Cape, 1968), p. 219.

32. Quoted in Ann Ware, ed., *Midwives of the Future* (Kansas City, Missouri: Leaven Press, 1985), p. 237.

33. M. K. Temerlin and J. W. Temerlin, "Psychotherapy Cults: An Iatrogenic Perversion," *Psychotherapy: Theory, Research and Practice,* 19:2 (1982), pp. 131–41.

34. Otto F. Kernberg, "Institutional Problems of Psychoanalytic Education," *Journal of the American Psychoanalytic Association,* 34 (1986), pp. 799–834.

35. Ibid.

36. Jacob A. Arlow, "Some Dilemmas in Psychoanalytic Education," *Journal of the American Psychoanalytic Association,* 20 (1972), pp. 556–566.

37. Ibid.

38. Irving Janis, *Victims of Groupthink* (Boston: Houghton Mifflin, 1972).

39. Arthur Schlesinger, *A Thousand Days* (Boston: Fawcett/ Houghton Mifflin, 1965) p. 259.

40. Stanley Milgram, *Obedience to Authority: An Experimental View* (San Francisco: Harper and Row, 1974).

41. Ibid., pp. 8–9.

42. Noam Chomsky quoted in William Barrett et al., "Human Rights and American Foreign Policy: A Symposium," *Commentary* 72 (November 1981), pp. 30–31.

CHAPTER 5: DEVALUING THE OUTSIDER

1. Jack Katz, *Seductions of Crime: Moral and Sensual Attractions in Doing Evil* (New York: Basic Books, 1988), pp. 36, 37.

2. Quoted in Al Santoli, *Everything We Had* (New York: Random House, 1981), p. 70.

3. *The American Psychiatric Association's Psychiatric Glossary*, ed. A. Werner et al. (Washington, D.C.: American Psychiatric Press, 1984), p. 110.

4. Hannah Arendt, *Eichmann in Jerusalem* (New York: Viking, 1963).

5. Stanley Milgram, *Obedience to Authority* (New York: Harper and Row, 1974).

6. Philip Zimbardo et al., "The Psychology of Imprisonment: Privation, Power and Pathology," in *Doing Unto Others: Explorations in Social Behavior*, ed. Z. Rubin (Englewood Cliffs, New Jersey: Prentice-Hall, 1974).

7. Quoted in Frances Fitzgerald, "A Reporter At Large: A Disciplined, Charging Army," *New Yorker*, 18 May 1981, p. 107.

8. Quoted in *Harper's Magazine*, April 1985, p. 17.

9. Quoted in *Harper's Magazine*, December 1983, p. 55.

10. Martin Marty, *A Nation of Believers* (Chicago: University of Chicago Press, 1976), pp. 81–82.

11. Todd Gitlin, *The Whole World Is Watching: Mass Media in the Making and Unmaking of the New Left* (Berkeley: University of California Press, 1980), p. 48 (note 22).

12. Ibid., p. 4.

13. Daniel Hallin, *The Uncensored War: The Media and Vietnam* (New York: Oxford University Press, 1982), p. 200.

14. Stephen Cohen, *Sovieticus: American Perceptions and Soviet Realities* (New York: W. W. Norton, 1985), pp. 29–30.

15. Herbert York, *The Advisers: Oppenheimer, Teller and the Superbomb* (San Francisco: W. H. Freeman, 1976), p. 34.

16. Philip Knightley, *The Second Oldest Profession: Spies and Spying in the Twentieth Century* (New York: W. W. Norton, 1986), pp. 264–265.

17. Robert Jervis, *Perception and Misperception in International Politics* (Princeton: Princeton University Press, 1976), p. 65.

18. Ibid., p. 61.

19. Ibid., p. 68.

20. Ibid., p. 61.

21. Peter H. Wyden, *Bay of Pigs: The Untold Story* (New York: Simon & Schuster, 1979), p. 8.

22. Quoted in Walter Capps, *The Unfinished War: Vietnam and the American Conscience*, 2d ed. (Boston: Beacon Press, 1990), pp. 92–93.

23. Ronald Reagan, Speech to the 41st Annual Convention of the National Association of Evangelicals, Orlando, Florida, 8 March 1983.

24. Ibid.

25. Jervis, p. 323.

26. Ibid., p. 328.

27. Randy Shilts, *And the Band Played On: People Politics and the AIDS Epidemic* (New York: St. Martin's Press, 1987).

28. Ibid., p. 335.

CHAPTER 6: AVOIDING DISSENT

1. Marc Galanter, "Psychological Induction Into the Large-Group: Findings from a Modern Religious Sect," *American Journal of Psychiatry* 137 (1980), pp. 1574–1579.

2. Ben Bagdikian, *The Media Monopoly*, 2d ed. (Boston: Beacon Press, 1987), pp. ix–x.

3. Ben Bagdikian, *The Media Monopoly* (Boston: Beacon Press, 1983).

4. Ibid., p. 24.

5. "NBC Snips Out Reference to GE," *San Francisco Chronicle*, 4 December 1989.

6. Bagdikian, 1987, pp. 27–39.

7. U.S. Bureau of Labor Statistics, cited in "Harper's Index," *Harper's Magazine*, August 1987, p. 11.

8. *Extra* 2:2, Sept/Oct 1988.

9. Bagdikian, 1987, p. 123.

10. George Gerbner et al., "Charting the Mainstream" in Doris Graber, ed. *Media Power in Politics* (Washington, D.C.: CQ Press, 1984), pp. 119–20.

11. Ibid., p. 129.

12. Ibid., p. 157.

13. Ibid., pp. 156–157.

14. Quoted in Ibid., pp. 171–172.

15. Ibid., p. 167.

16. Ibid., p. 155.

17. Bernard Roshco, *Newsmaking* (Chicago: University of Chicago Press, 1975), p. 115.

18. Warren Weaver, *Both Your Houses* (New York: Praeger Publishers, 1972), p. 12.

19. Mark Hertsgaard, *On Bended Knee: The Press and the Reagan Presidency* (New York: Schocken Books, 1988), p. 347.

20. *Extra* 2:4, Jan/Feb 1989.

21. Quoted in Robert Stein, *Media Power: Who Is Shaping Your Picture of the World?* (Boston: Houghton Mifflin, 1972), p. 30.

22. Hallin, p. 50.

23. Ibid., p. 208.

24. David Altheide, "Iran vs. U.S. TV News: The Hostage Story out of Context," in Doris Graber, ed., *Media Power in Politics*, p. 300.

25. Hallin, p. 99.

26. Edward Herman and Noam Chomsky, *Manufacturing Consent—The Political Economy of the Mass Media* (New York: Pantheon, 1988), p. 348.

27. Herbert Gans, *Deciding What's News—A Study of CBS Evening News, NBC Nightly News, Newsweek, and Time* (New York: Pantheon, 1979), p. 277.

28. Bagdikian, 1987, p. 218.

29. Quoted in Wright, pp. 42, 47.

30. Ibid., pp. 65–66.

31. Byron, p. 105.

32. Ibid., p. 201.

33. Henry Cooper, Jr., "Letter From The Space Center," *New Yorker*, 10 November 1986.

34. Wyden, pp. 148–149.

35. *San Francisco Chronicle*, 20 August 1986.

36. Ibid.

37. Conway and Siegelman, p. 86.

38. Streiker, p. 91.

39. Conway and Siegelman, p. 144.

40. Elizabeth Bugental, private communication to the author.

41. M. Wong, *Nun: A Memoir* (New York: Harcourt Brace Jovanovich, 1983), p. 300.

42. Liz Harris, "Holy Days," *New Yorker*, 30 September 1985, p. 88.

43. Deikman, "The Evaluation of Spiritual and Utopian Groups."

44. Tom Wicker, *On Press—A Top Reporter's Life in, and Reflections on, American Journalism* (New York: Viking, 1978), p. 195.

CHAPTER 7: ESCAPE FROM CULT THINKING

1. Quoted in Robert McNamara, "The Military Role of Nuclear Weapons," *Foreign Affairs*, Fall 1983.

2. Hyman Rickover, in testimony during congressional hearings of the Joint Economic Committee, reported in *Rolling Stone*, 1 April 1982.

3. Quoted in *San Francisco Chronicle*, 9 May 1982.

4. William Morris, ed., *The American Heritage Dictionary*, p. 474.

5. Barbara Tuchman, *The March of Folly* (New York: Alfred A. Knopf, 1984), p. 7.

6. Ibid., p. 32.

7. Quoted in B. Berelson, P. Lazarfeld and W. McPhee, *Voting: A Study of Opinion Formation in a Presidential Campaign* (Chicago: University of Chicago Press, 1954), pp. 314–315.

8. Ibid.

9. Jacques Ellul, *Propaganda: The Formation of Men's Attitudes* (New York: Knopf, 1965).

10. Ibid.

11. Geneen, pp. 133–134.

12. Pascale and Athos, p. 97.

13. Ibid., p. 110.

14. Ibid., pp. 269, 270.

15. William Manchester, *American Caesar: Douglas MacArthur 1880–1964* (Boston: Little, Brown and Co., 1978), p. 215.

16. Janis, pp. 209–215.

17. Ibid., pp. 138–149.

18. Ibid., p. 150.

19. Ibid., p. 152.

20. Quoted in George Lardner, Jr., "The Tower Report Sows a Mine Field

for the Administration," *Washington Post National Weekly Edition*, 9 March 1987, p. 13.

21. "D-Day veterans remember their baptism by fire," *San Francisco Sunday Examiner and Chronicle*, 3 June 1984.

22. Mohandas Gandhi, *Non-Violent Resistance* (Satyagraha) (New York: Schocken Books, 1961), p. 193.

23. Louis Fischer, *The Life of Gandhi* (New York: Harper & Brothers, 1950), p. 117.

24. Erik Erikson, *Gandhi's Truth* (New York: W. W. Norton, 1969).

25. Robert McNamara, *Introduction to Robert Kennedy's Thirteen Days* (New York: W. W. Norton, 1969), pp. 14–15.

26. Janis, pp. 159–160.

27. Janis, p. 164.

CHAPTER 8: THE TERRORIST THREAT

1. Rohan Gunaratna, *Inside Al Qaeda: Global Network of Terror* (New York: Columbia University Press, 2002), p. 7.

2. Ibid., p. 85.

3. Mark Juergensmeyer, *Terror in the Mind of God—The Global Rise of Religious Violence* (Berkely: University of California Press, 2000), p. 155.

4. Ibid., p. 243

5. Robert J. Lifton, *Destroying the World to Save It—Aum Shinrikyo, Apocalyptic Violence, and the New Global Terrorism,* (New York: Henry Holt, 1999).

6. Gail Luft, *Foreign Affairs,* (July/August, 2002), p. 2–7.

7. Ben Bagdikian, *The Media Monopoly*, (Boston: Beacon Press, 1983), p. xvi.

8. Juergensmeyer, op. cit., p. 165.

9. Nicholas Lernam, "What terrorists want," *New Yorker,* 29 October 2001, p. 41.

10. Malise Ruthven, *A Fury for God—The Islamist Attack on America,* (London: Granta Books, 2002), p. 288.

11. Scott Peterson, "In war some facts less factual," *Christian Science Monitor*, 6 September 2002, p. 14.

12. Gunaratna, op. cit., p. 232.

13. Lifton, op. cit., p. 342

14. Ruthven, op. cit., p. 283.

15. Daniel Pipes, *Militant Islam Reaches America,* (New York: W.W. Norton, 2002), p. 56.

16. Pipes, op. cit., p. 57.

17. Alan Dershowitz, *Why Terrorism Works,* (New Haven: Yale University Press, 2002).

18. Ruthven, op. cit., p.27.

19. David Hoffman, "Beyond Public Diplomacy," *Foreign Affairs*, March/April 2002, p. 88.

20. Hoffman, op. cit., p. 93.

Index

Abortion, 79; anti—, 175
Abrams, Eliot, 135
Adelman, Kenneth, 178. *See also* Arms Control and Disarmament Agency
Advertising, 128–29, 132
Afghanistan, 78, 122, 174
"Ageism," 76
A. H. Robbins Company, 72
AIDS epidemic, 124–25
al Qaeda, 173; attraction to Holy War, 177; opposition within, 181–82; propaganda, 184; suicide bombers, 182; avoiding cult thinking, 185
Al-Jazeera, 183
Allende, Salvador, 145, 167
Altheide, David, 137
Amayreh, Khalid M., 181. *See also* Middle East conflict
American Broadcasting Company (ABC), 116, 135
American Legion, 148
American Psychoanalytic Association, 99
Americans United, 93

Anger, 104, 112
Annenberg School of Communication, 130
Anti-nuclear movement, 63–64, 116–17, 150–52, 161
Anxiety, 16, 53, 77, 92, 101, 103, 109. *See also* Fear
Arendt, Hannah, 110
Argentina, 144
Arlow, Jacob, 100
Arms Control and Disarmament Agency, 178
Army, U. S., 57, 70. *See also* Military
Asbestos, 72
AT&T, 64, 69, 89
Athos, Anthony, 71, 160
Atta, Mohammed, 184
Aum cult in Tokyo, Japan, 173. *See also* Lifton, Robert
Authoritarianism. *See* Leaders, authoritarian
Autonomy, 60, 75–76

"Baby Jane Doe" case, 79
Bagdikian, Ben, 127–29, 132, 139, 177

Bakker, Jim, 115
Ball, George, 167
Bandura, Albert, 55
Banking, 78, 149
Bay of Pigs operation, 101–2, 120, 161–63, 167
Bendana, Alejandro, 135
Bennet, Arthur, 125
Bible, 91, 176, 179
Bin Laden, Osama, 172–75
Bion, Wilfred, 57–58
Branch Davidians, 173, 175–76
Bright, Bill, 95
Britain, 120, 123
Brodeur, Paul, 72
Buddhism, 89
Bundy, McGeorge, 78, 141, 162
Bush, George, 137
Bush, George W., 154; Middle East conflict, 178–79; response to September 11, 179
Business world, 11, 84–85, 123, 131. *See also* Banking; Corporations
Byron, Christopher, 87

Caligula, 84
Cambodia, 117, 136, 167
Camp David, 80
Campus Crusade, 95
Carlson, Ed, 160
Carter, Jimmy, 78, 80, 137
Castro, Fidel, 120; anti—, 101
Catholicism, 71, 114, 142–43. *See also* Christianity
Celebrities, 75, 115
Censorship, 117, 126–27, 129, 134, 149, 183; de facto, 149, 177; lower-level, 141; self—, 135–36; Christian fundamentalists and, 91, 93, 95, 111, 114–15, 124, 142–43, 179; in Iran, 176. *See also* Dissent
Challenger shuttle disaster, 141

Chastity, 59
Chicago Tribune, 128
Child:—birth, 8, 39;—care, 54, 60–61, 66, 76–77; parent—, relation. *See* Dependency; Family
Chile, 145
China, 61, 118, 136
Chomsky, Noam, 106, 129, 137–38
Christ: anti—, 32, 50; belief in, and members of the Life Force group, 38, 43, 45, 51; love of, Falwell on, 93, 95, 111; surrender to, 61, 94; worship of, and fundamentalist leadership, 95, 111, 179
Christianity, 62, 91, 111, 179; and the avoidance of dissent, 142–44; and the devaluation of outsiders, 113–15. *See also* Catholicism; Fundamentalism; Protestantism
Cialdini, Robert, 56
Class differences, 130, 152; corporate, 86; government; 134
Cohen, Stephen, 118
Cold War ideology, 118–19, 136
Colman, Arthur, 58
Columbia Broadcasting Service (CBS), 115–16; broadcasting, 132, 138, 176–77, 184
Communism, 106, 118, 132, 136–37; Chinese, 148; overthrow of, as a political cause, 166; Russian, 148
Concorde, 123
Conformity, 54, 59, 87–88, 138, 143, 146, 148
Conscience, 7, 77, 94. *See also* Morality
Consciousness, 58, 62–63; altered states of, 7, 62; youthful, 76. *See also* Dependency, dreams
Constitution, 12; First Amendment of, 127, 129, 177
Contras, 72, 79–80, 163

Conversion, 61, 75; and corporate culture, 53, 68–69; and idealism, 63, 84–85; and psychoanalytic education, 99; and validation of the leader, 6, 52, 57, 62. *See also* Consciousness, altered states of; Initiation

Cooper, Henry, Jr., 141

Cooperman, Alan, 176

Corporations, 11, 52–53, 65–72,; as big "parents," 72; and "corporate culture," 68–72; decision making in, 84–85; and dissent, 137–41, 159–63; "excellent, " Peters and Waterman on, 84–85; generation of "fervor" in, 70–73, 80; Japanese, 70; and the Life Force group, parallels between, 88, 137; managers of, economic dependence of, 65; marriages and, 62, 65–68; and the media, 127–133, 128, 135–39; religious tone of, 71–72; and the use of overwork, 67–68, 70

Correll, Thomas, 15, 19, 25

Corvair fiasco, 139–40

Couples, separation of, 8, 30, 59–60, 112; at a Buddhist seminary; 82–83; and the Life Force group, 30–47;

Crusades, 114

Cuba: the Bay of Pigs operation, 101, 118, 138, 141, 162–63, 169; the Cuban Missile Crisis, 101, 161–62, 167–68

Curran, Charles Reverand, 142

Dalkon shield, 72

Damnation, 6, 36, 46, 50, 96, 110–11, 113, 170, 179

Davidians. *See* Branch Davidians

Deal, Terrance, 71

De Lorean, John, 86, 139

Delta Airlines, 69

Democracy, 12, 79, 142; facade of, among cults, 25; Falwell on, 142; principles of, and Japanese internment camps, 105, 166; voting and, 157

Dependency, 2, 8–12, 72–100, 171–73;—assumption group, Bion on, 57; authority—, relationships, Rioch on, 73; and compliance with groups, 59–63; definition of, 8; as a primitive emotional state, 57; and psychotherapy, 97–98; and reference groups, 54; unresolved, and guided fantasies, 18, 62; —dreams, 53, 169, 173; and the four basic behaviors found in cults, 52–53; and leaders, 75–76, 78–84, 90; saviour fantasies, 95, 98; superparent fantasy, 77, 79, 80–84, 185

Dershowitz, Alan, 182

Devil, 13, 46, 110. *See also* Evil

Dillon, Douglas, 162, 167

Dissent, 22, 24, 52–53, 105, 126–49; and censorship, 115, 127–39; and loyalty, 139–42; and the media, 127–38; promotion of, 166–69; punishment of, 32, 83, 127; and religion, 143–45

Doctors, 70, 150

Dowie, Mark, 129

Dreams, dependency. *See* Dependency, dreams

Drug treatment, 99

Dulles, John F., 120

Education, 6, 11, 13–14; anti-authoritarian, 156; fundamentalism and, 143; psychoanalytic, 99–100; terrorism, 180–81, 184

Edwards, Harry, 135

Eichmann, Adolf, 110
Ellul, Jacques, 158
El Salvador, 137
Empathy, 56, 110
Equal Rights Amendment, 131
Erikson, Erik, 166
Ethics, professional, 99. *See also*
  Morality
Ethnic groups, 110, 135, 138, 143, 149,
  173, 177
Evil, 13, 33, 80, 110–11, 142, 149, 153;
  beliefs regarding, in the Life
  Force group, 27–46; "the elemental" as, 27, 31–32; "empire"
  speech, Reagan's, 121–22, 147;
  feelings of rebellion as, 104;
  "freedom" from, 28; and righteousness, feelings of, 154–55. *See
  also* Goodness
Evolution, 58, 105
Excommunication, 8
Exit: from cults, 150–70; and contact with outsiders, 127; and evil,
  "giving in to," 33; and excommunication, 8; and exit from
  corporations, 64–65; from the
  Life Force group, 43, 49–51;
  from the Peoples Temple, 6, 11;
  punishment of, 8; and understanding cult behavior, 11

Falwell, Reverend Jerry, 88, 91–92,
  111, 135, 142
Families: banding together of, for
  mutual protection, 58; of corporate managers, 65–68; cults as, 3,
  11; and religious exclusiveness,
  111;—breaking up of, 3, 5–6, 59;
  and the Life Force group, 4–54.
  See also Family
Family, 52, 87; backgrounds, of
  devotees, 5; the father and, 16–
  17, 54, 74, 175; nuclear, 65; and

reference groups, 54; structure,
  and leaders, 74–77, 83, 139,
  159–60; and the devaluation
  of outsiders, 110. *See also*
  Families
Father, 9, 16–17, 35, 50, 54, 74, 80,
  84, 169. *See also* Family
FBI, 175. *See also* Branch
  Davidians
Fear: and departure, from cults, 45–
  51; of abandonment, 63, 169; of
  dogs, 55; of growing old, 76; of
  leaders, 7–8, 49, 53, 86–88; of
  punishment, 96; and propa-
  ganda, 157; and projection, 110.
  See also Anxiety
Federal Communications Commission (FCC), 129–30
Federal Trade Commission (FTC),
  129–30
Fight-flight response, 57
Financial exploitation, of devotees,
  5, 7, 59
Food and Drug Administration
  (FDA), 133
France, 164
Freed, Fred, 136
Freedom, 2–3, 77, 89, 95, 104, 162,
  172; and democracy, 12, 177, 184;
  from evil, 91, 147; and the media,
  128, 132, 148
Freud, Sigmund, 56–57, 97, 100
Fromm, Erich, 86
Fundamentalism, 85–86, 88–89;
  and AIDS, 121; and censorship,
  142–43; and the devaluation of
  outsiders, 105, 107, 121

Gandhi, Mahatma, 44, 74, 90, 165–
  68
Gans, Herbert, 138
Gay rights activists. *See*
  Homosexuality

Geneen, Harold, 68, 86, 159–60
General Electric (GE), 84, 128
General Motors (GM), 72, 86, 139, 166
Genocide, 106, 182
Germany, 61, 77–78, 114, 123, 148; youth of, after World War II, 148, 161. *See also* Nazism
Gitlin, Todd, 116–17
God, 9, 13, 50, 61, 93–96, 113–14; belief in, and the silencing of dissent, 141–42, 144, 181, 185; call of, vs. institutional callings, 96–97; and goodness, 142; intuition of, 95; obedience to, 90–92; punishment by, and AIDS, 124; will of, and righteousness, 70, 106, 177
Goodness, 80, 86, 160, 168; and God, 143; and self-righteousness, 105, 118. *See also* Evil
Gorbachev, Mikhail, 118
Government, 52, 78, 101, 103, 106, 118–25, 127–29, 145–47, 161; on terrorism, 166, 172, 184; U.S., 175. *See also* Leaders, political
Graham, Billy, 145
Guatemala, 137
Gunaratna, Rohan, 172; helping Arab and Muslim states, 180

Haig, Alexander, 135
Hallaj, 142
Hallin, Daniel, 117–18, 136–37
Hamilton, Lee, 180
Harris, Liz, 94, 144
Hasidic communities, 94, 144
Heresy, 142, 149
Herman, Edward, 137–38
Hertsgaard, Mark, 134
Hickey, Archbishop, 142
Hinduism, 90, 96, 114, 166, 176
Hitler, Adolf, 74, 81, 85, 171

Hitler Youth, 61, 71
Hoffman, David, Western-style objective journalism, 183–84
Holy War, 171, 177; and preservation of self-image, 181
Home, Lord, 78
Homosexuality, 124–25
Humanism, 143
Human potential movement, 16
Houssein, Saddam, 175. *See also* Taliban; al Qaeda

IBM, 69, 71
Idi Amin, 84
India, 90
Individuation, 58
Indochina, 137
Initiations, 62–63, 70, 100
Iran, 78, 90, 112; censorship in, 143; —contra scandal, 72, 80, 163, 167; hostage crisis, 137
Islam, 91, 115, 172, 174–75, 179, 181–82
ITT, 68, 86, 159–60

Jackson, Jesse, 135
Janis, Irving, 101, 145, 161
Japan, 70, 105, 161, 167, 173, 180; corporations in, 71
Jervis, Robert, 119–20, 123
Jesus. *See* Christ
Jihad. *See* Holy War
Johns Mansville company, 72
John Paul II, Pope, 142
Johnson, Nicholas, 129
Johnson, Samuel, 103–4
Joint Chiefs of Staff, 151–52, 160
Jones, Jim, 173
Jones, Reginald, 84
Jonestown, Guyana. *See* Peoples Temple
Judaism, 91, 111, 113–14, 144, 154, 171, 174, 176, 178–79

Juergensmeyer, Mark, 172–73, 177
Juvenile delinquents, 108

Kaiser Aluminum, 87
Kanter, Rosabeth, 60
Karpel, Craig, 77–78
Kassenbaum, Nancy, 163
Katz, Jack, 108
Kaunda, Kenneth D., 165
Kennedy, Allen, 71
Kennedy, John F., 101–2, 117, 161–62, 167
Kennedy, Robert, 102, 162, 167–68
Kernberg, Otto, 99–100
Khomeini, Ayatollah, 112
Khrushchev, Nikita, 93, 120
King, Martin Luther, Jr., 93, 165
Kirkpatrick, Jean, 135
Kissinger, Henry, 78, 135
Klein, Melanie, 57
Kohl, Helmut, 78
Kollwitz, Kathe, 44
Koran, 91, 172, 179, 184
Korean War, 148, 160
Koresh, David. *See* Branch Davidians

Latin America, 137–38
LaRocque, Gene, 151
Leaders, 16, 18, 71, 86–87, 141–43; anger at, displacement of, 110; charismatic, 2, 11, 74–75, 83, 163; critical evaluation of, suppression of, 7–8, 74; dependency on, 2, 11, 73, 104. *See also* Dependency; fear of, 7, 52–53, 93; guidance of, and freedom from evil, 31–32; and omnipotence, 57, 76–77, 80, 101; as parent figures, 5, 7, 52, 60, 79–80; personality of, 74; and psychotherapists, comparison of, 97–99; special knowledge pos-

sessed by, and special authority, 25; spiritual power of, and altered states of consciousness, 56; "transforming," 83; validation of, during the introductory phase, 5; —authoritarian, 7, 9, 52, 74–77, 106, 157, 169; and the child/parent relationship, 74, 80, 97, 141, 161–63; in corporations, 84–92, 141–42; and devaluation of outsiders, 104; Fromm on, 86; and presidential leadership, 101; religious, 93–95, 110, 145; —political, 58, 70–80; Barber on, 79; and the Bilderberg Meeting, 78–79; as celebrities, 74; and the concept of national interest, 106; and dissent, 147–49, 159–68; invulnerability of, fantasy of, 101; "superiority" of, fantasy of, 52, 77, 82, 107, 143; and the unwillingness to acknowledge one's own evil, 121–22. *See also* Life Force group, leadership of
Le Bon, Gustave, 56
Legionnaire's Disease, 124–25
Lewis, C. S., 122
Liberalism, 59, 63, 111, 130, 147, 149, 153, 155, 157
Life Force group, 14–43, 97, 134–35, 147, 157–58, 185; beliefs regarding evil in, 30–36; and corporate culture, parallels between, 88, 140; and "cutting," procedure of, 34–35, 40; and families, breaking up of, 22–23, 26–27, 30–31, 34–44; notion of "group mind" in, 26–28; quarantine procedure and, 31–32, 41, 45; secrecy and, 30, 145–46; —leadership of, 14–50, 52, 57, 74–75, 103–4; and

initiation to the inner circle of
the Center, 101; and omnipotence, 80–81; and paranoia, 46,
48, 58, 80–81
Lifton, Robert, 2–3, 180
Loory, Stuart, 133
Love, 9, 14, 31, 44, 49, 53, 57, 59–
60, 74, 80, 111
Luft, Gail, 174

MacArthur, Douglas, 160–61
McCarthy era, 148; McCarthyism,
93
McNamara, Robert, 162, 167
Mahler, Margaret, 58
Malcolm, Janet, 55
Manchester, William, 160
Mao Tse-tung, 61, 81
Margolis, Diane, 65
Marriage, 59–60, 68. *See also*
Couples, separation of
Maslow, Abraham, 122–23
Media, 4, 52, 111, 135–38; advertis-
ing, 129–32; and AIDS, 124; and
celebrities, status of, 71, 115; cor-
porations and, 128–30, 139–43;
devaluation of outsiders in, 104,
114–15, 117, 124; and dissent,
127–38; and government au-
thority, 134–39; and objectivity,
117, 133–34; political commen-
tary, 157, 164; radio talk shows,
108, 111, 115; treatment of student
dissidents, 116–18. *See also*
Television
Meditation, 7
Meier, Cornelle, 87
Meshad, Shad, 121
Messiah, 62, 179. *See also* Christ
MGM, 132
Middle East conflict, 178–79;
seeking self-respect, 181; suicide

bombers, 182. *See also* September
11
Milgram, Stanley, 104–5, 110
Military, 64, 70, 105, 111, 119, 131,
136, 148, 150–55, 180; the Bay of
Pigs operation, 101–2, 120, 161–
63, 167; the bombing of Pearl
Harbor, 79, 105, 167; the Cuban
Missile Crisis, 101, 161–62, 167–
68. *See also* Nuclear war
Mohammed, 90
Morality, 71, 108, 139, 146, 156, 166–
67; and corporate culture, 71,
139; and devaluation of outsiders,
112, 121; and God's call, 96–97,
185; and psychotherapy, 145
Morgan Guaranty, 69
Moslims, 111, 113, 142, 154, 171, 173,
176, 180, 183–84
Munro, Richard, 87
Mussolini, Benito, 153

National Broadcasting Company
(NBC), 116, 128, 136
National interest, concept of, 106
Nationalism, 118–19
Nazism, 61, 71, 171, 182
New York Psychoanalytic Institute,
55
Nicaragua, 79, 138
Nicodemus, 61
Nitze, Paul, 141
Nixon, Richard, 84, 133, 145
North, Oliver, 72
Nuclear energy, 72, 117, 151
Nuclear war, 2, 63–64, 101, 117,
150–52, 154, 161
Nursery schools, 55

Objectivity, 117, 134
Object relations theory, 58
O'Connor, Robert, 55

Oneida community, 60
Orwell, George, 83
Outsiders, devaluation of, 7, 52–53, 107–11, 127, 149, 170, and AIDS, 124; and foreign affairs, 111, 173; in the media, 115–18, 124; and nationalism, 111, 170–71, 173; and projection, reliance upon, 36, 98, 107–11, 152, 154–55, 164; and psychiatry, 52, 114, 164; and self-righteousness, 113, 143, 156; and violence, 111, 173
Overwork, use of, 70

Palmerston, Lord, 120
Paranoia, 8, 141, 152–53; and the devaluation of others, 123; in the Life Force group, 46, 48
Parent-child relation. *See* Dependency; Family
Pascale, Richard, 71, 160
Patriotism, 104, 146
Peace movement, 64–65, 151–53
Pearl Harbor, 79, 105–6, 167
Pentagon, 130, 135, 145
Peoples Temple of San Francisco, 5–6, 12; mass suicide in Guyana, 6, 11–12, 53, 173
Peters, Thomas, 71, 84, 86
Physicians for Social Responsibility, 64, 151
Pillar, Paul, regarding terrorists, 180
Pipes, Daniel, fascism and Marism-Leninism, 181. *See also* Middle East conflict
Poland, 138, 148
Political groups, 104, 161–62; antinuclear movement, 63; conservative, 95, 114, 135, 147, 149, 153, 155; left-wing, 135; liberal, 63, 111, 130, 147, 149, 153, 155, 157; opposition of, and devaluation of outsiders, 114, 164; Physicians for

Social Responsibility, 64, 151; right-wing, 63, 135, 153
Political leaders. *See* Leaders, political
Political science, 79, 104, 146, 186
Polk, James, 119–20
Popieluszko, Jerszy, 137
Procter & Gamble, 69, 130–32
Projection, 36, 98, 107–11, 152, 154–55, 164
Prostitution, 5
Protestantism, 114. *See also* Christianity
Psychic ability, 61
Psychotherapy, 2, 16, 97–99; and avoiding dissent, 126, 145, 174, 185; and devaluation of outsiders, 52, 114, 164; and drug treatment, use of, 91, 99
Puckett, R. G., 93
Puerperal fever, 112
Punishment, 119, 176; in corporate cultures, 86–87; of dissent, 7, 32, 83, 126, 176; and extreme dependence, nature of, 59, 75; fear of, 90–91, 96, 106, 109, 114, 142; of religious persecution, 124
Purpose, sense of, 6–7, 19–20, 27, 71, 78, 84, 92, 112, 166, 173. *See also* World, "saving the"

Rabi, Isador, 113
Racial differences, 6, 110, 130
Radio: shortwave, 119; talk shows, 64, 108, 111, 115, 127, 129–30, 147, 157, 183
Reagan, Ronald (Reagan administration), 77, 79–80, 134–35, 145, 178; "evil empire" speech, 121–22, 147; and the Iran-contra scandal, 72, 80, 145; and Latin America, 79, 137, 152; and the media, 134–35, 137

Rebellion, 26, 70, 100
Reincarnation, 33, 90
Religion, 4, 11, 52; avoiding dissent, 142, 145; and authoritarian leadership, 91–93; Branch Davidians, 175; corporate, 70–71; and devaluation of outsiders, 114, 164; and intuitive capacity, 95–96; and the primal horde, in Freud, 56; terror-based, 185–86; theistic, 89. *See also* specific religions
Revivalism, 61
Righteousness, 65, 70, 72, 84, 111, 113, 120, 122, 148, 154–55, 166–67, 176, 182
Rioch, Margaret, 72, 80
Rituals, 93, 144
Rockefeller, David, 78
Romans, ancient, 82
Roosevelt, Kermit, 129
Roshco, Bernard, 133
Rusk, Dean, 141, 162, 168
Ruthven, Malise, 178

Saint John of the Cross, 89–90
SANE, 116–17
"Satanization," 173
Schizophrenia, 46
Schlesinger, Arthur, 102
Schlumberger, 67, 70, 160
Schmidt, Helmut, 78
Schultz, Reverend Wallace, 176
Sears, Roebuck, 128
Secrecy, 30, 88
Self-esteem, 7, 127; lack of, and extreme dependence, 59; sources of, in the corporate world, 65
Selfishness, 23, 26–27, 32–33, 60, 83, 96, 140, 165, 178
Semmelweis, I. P., 112
Separatism, 5, 152
September 11, 171, 174–75, 184
Sexuality, 5, 8, 59–61, 98, 124, 142

Shah, Idries, 91–92
Shilts, Randy, 124–25
Shock experiments, 104
Sleep deprivation, 42, 47, 62, 70, 163
Sloan, Alfred, 86
Smuts, John, 166
Socialist Party, 148. *See also* Communism
Socialization, 68–69
Sorensen, Theodore, 162
Soul, 13, 32, 90
South Africa, 166
Soviet Union, 78, 118, 120–21; and the Cuban Missile Crisis, 161, 168. *See also* Cuban Missile Crisis; and Reagan's "evil empire" speech, 132, 138
Sports, 75
Sputnik, 119
Stalin, Joseph, 81, 106, 121, 171
Sterilization, 5
Stockman, David, 79
Street gangs, 108
Streiker, Lowell, 61
Students for a Democratic Society (SDS), 116
Suicide: mass, 5–6, 71; bomber, 181–82
Surrender: as a basic feature of spiritual life, 62, 94–95; childlike, to the parent/family group, 37; to Christ, 62, 94–95; images of, 5
Survival, human, 58, 63, 74, 168
Survivalists, 64
Swaggart, Jimmy, 115

Taliban, 175
Tavistock Group Relations Conference, 72, 102
Television, 75, 115–16, 118; and avoidance of dissent, 130–31;

Television *(continued)*
commentary, political, 153, 160;
entertainment programs, violence
in, 147, 153–54; homogenizing
effect of, 130, 133; networks, 115–
18; religious broadcasting, 108;
the *Television-Cable Week* fiasco,
140. *See also* Media

Terrorism, 4, 166, 171–74, 178–79,
181, 185

Theresa, Mother, 43–44

Thiokol, 141

Third Reich, 61, 71

Thirty Year War, 114

Time, Inc., 87, 139–40

Timerman, Jacobo, 144

Totalitarianism, 87–88, 140

Transference, 3, 98

Tribune Company, 128

Truman, Harry S., 119

Tuchman, Barbara, 156

Tylenol capsule crisis, 125

Underwood, Barbara, 95

Unification Church, 70, 95

United Airlines, 160

Utilitarianism, 56

Utopian rehabilitation group, 6

Values, 167; and corporate culture,
68–69, 139; and obedience to
God, 91, 93; spiritual, and life
force psychology, 19

Vatican, 142

Vietnam War, 105–6, 121; media
coverage of, 136–37; protests
against, 117–18

Violence, 3, 108; and devaluation
of outsiders, 105–6, 108, 121;
vulnerability to, and dependency
dreams, 9, 52–53

Voice of America (VOA), 183

Warsaw Pact, 78

Watergate scandal, 84

Waterman, Robert, Jr., 71, 86

Weaver, Warren, 134

Weinberger, Caspar, 151

Whalen, Edith, 131

Wicker, Tom, 146

Wilentz, Sean, 181

Wilson, Charles Edward, 72, 84

Winnicott, D. W., 58

World, "saving the," 7, 72, 82, 85;
and the Life Force group, 13, 18–
21, 34, 44, 104, 170

World Trade Center, "attack on,"
171. *See also* September 11

World War I, 123

World War II, 148, 161, 171. *See also*
Nazism

Wyden, Peter H., 120–21, 141

Yoga, 62

Zambia, 165

Zilg, Gerard, 129

Zimbardo, Philip, 110